NATURAL
WONDERS
of North America

BY CATHERINE O'NEILL

BOOKS FOR WORLD EXPLORERS
NATIONAL GEOGRAPHIC SOCIETY

CONTENTS

Copyright © 1984 National Geographic Society
Library of Congress CIP data: page 104

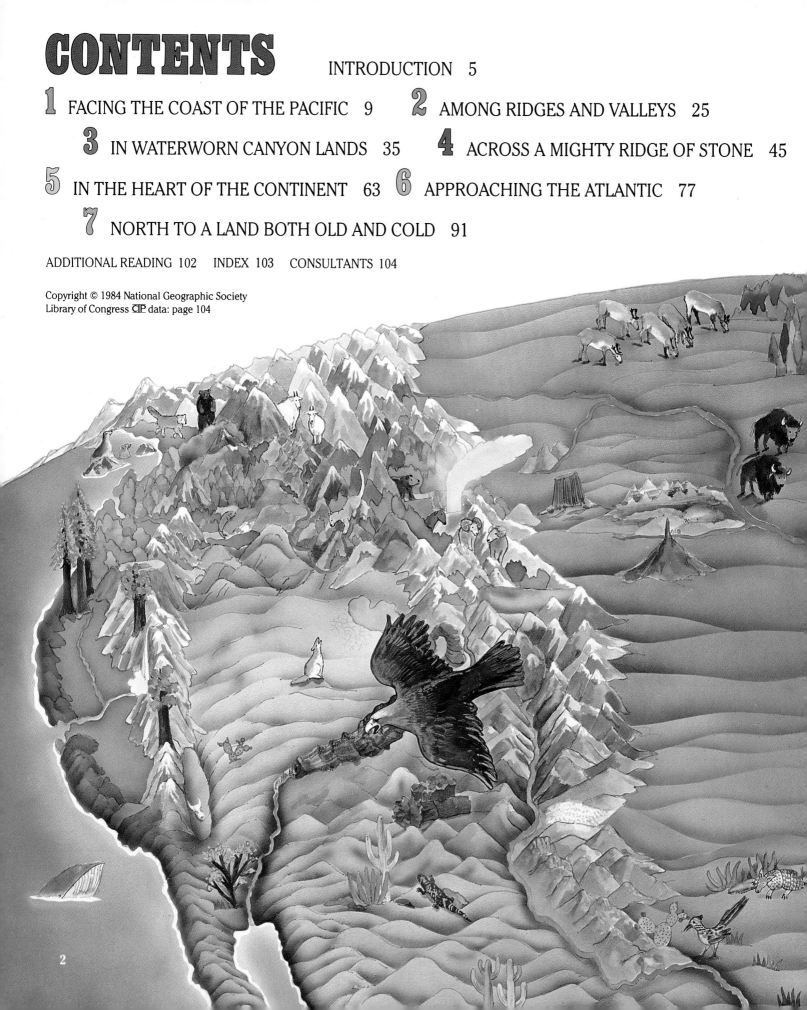

Can you find Devils Tower below? How about Crater Lake? Do you see Delicate Arch? Redwood trees? Lake Superior? Chimney Rock? Cape Hatteras? Petrified trees? Niagara Falls? Don't worry if you can't find all these features right now. When you reach the end of the book, the natural wonders shown in this painting of North America will be familiar to you.

GLORIA MARCONI

TITLE PAGE: *Delicate Arch throws its shadow across the red sandstone of Arches National Park, in eastern Utah. The 85-foot-high (26-m) stone arch is one of more than 300 naturally formed arches in the park.*

TOM AND PAT LEESON

COVER: *From the North Rim of the Grand Canyon, three visitors look out over the largest gorge on earth. Far below them, the Colorado River flows along the course it has carved during the past ten million years.*

WILBUR E. GARRETT, NATIONAL GEOGRAPHIC STAFF

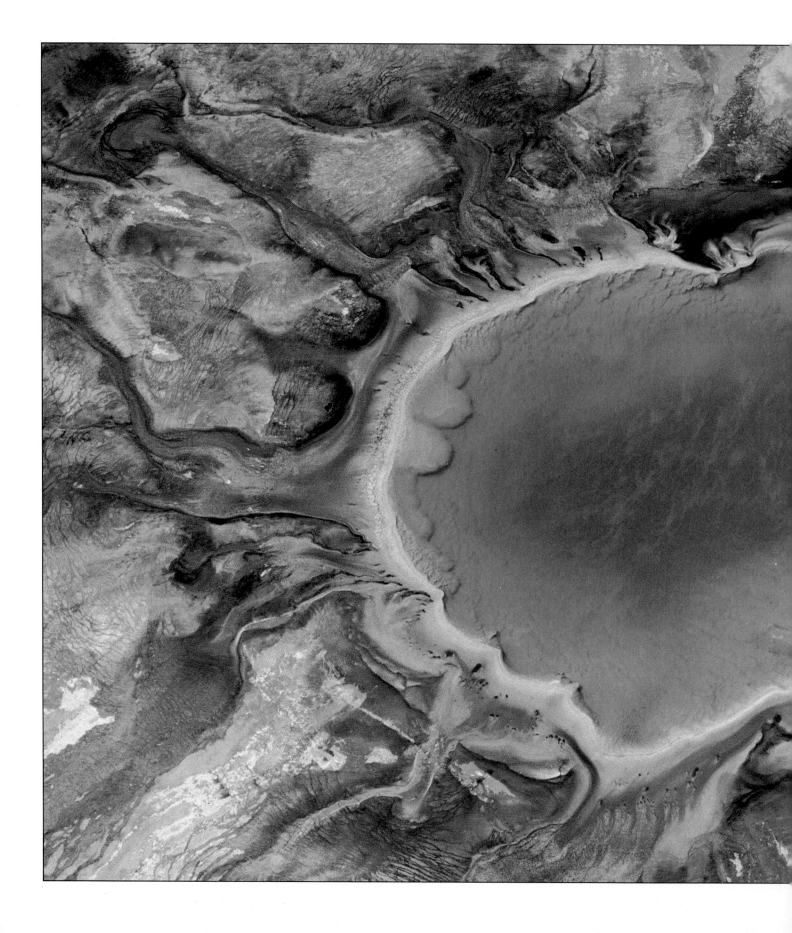

Colorful plants called algae (AL-jee) ring the edges of Grand Prismatic Spring, in Yellowstone National Park, in Wyoming (left). Nothing grows at the center, where the water simmers at 167°F (75°C)* —hotter than you could touch. Tourists walk past on a boardwalk built for safety. Yellowstone Park contains thousands of hot springs and spouting geysers. They are heated by superhot melted rock called magma below the surface of the ground. These natural wonders attract millions of visitors every year.
GEORG GERSTER

"Natural wonders"—the words suggest many things, from towering redwood trees on the West Coast to sandy beaches on the Atlantic shore. What do you think of when you hear the words? You may imagine an underground chamber in Mammoth Cave, or the wind-whipped peak of Mount Washington, or the wide waters of the Mississippi River. You'll certainly think of the Grand Canyon.

The North American continent contains a large variety of natural formations, "wonders" created by the powers of nature. Some have been built up by forces within the earth. Others have been carved by rain and ice and other outside forces working directly on the earth's surface.

Geologists, scientists who study the earth and its movements, believe the earth is made up of layers of mostly rocky and metallic material. They call the outer layer the crust. The crust is broken into enormous pieces called plates. These make up the continents and the ocean floors. The plates rest on a thick layer of partly melted rock called the upper mantle. Heat from within the earth produces very slow currents in the upper mantle. The currents cause the plates to shift, and the shifting causes changes in the surface features of earth's crust.

Most changes in the earth's crust occur too slowly for you to notice. It's impossible to feel North America drift. The continent moves only about an inch (2½ cm) a year. You might witness one of the more dramatic changes, such as an earthquake or a volcanic eruption. But most of the landforms you see result from millions of years of extremely slow change.

To explore some of the spectacular results of nature's work, turn the pages of this book.

*Metric figures in this book have been rounded off.

You may have put together a jigsaw puzzle map showing the United States, Canada, and Mexico. As you put the map together, you became familiar with the shape of the state or province where you live. That shape shows the land divided along a political boundary—a boundary decided upon by governments.

Scientists can agree on another kind of boundary, one based on the geology, or land formations, of an area. On the smaller map at right, you see the major physical features of North America. Mountain ranges stretch along the West and East Coasts. Wide plains extend in between. Some geologists divide the continent into regions on the basis of how these and other natural features were formed. The larger map shows seven such regions. Each one is a different color. The black lines show political boundaries of Canada, the United States, and Mexico.

Chapter by chapter in this book, you will travel to these seven different geologic regions of North America. You will start in the region that formed most recently, the West Coast. Giant glaciers and steep volcanic peaks rise before you. Next you hike up and down the mountains and valleys that form the Basin and Range and Mexican Highlands. Several canyons of the Colorado Plateau, including the Grand Canyon, fall away at your feet. You then turn north, toward the towering Rockies and the neighboring Columbia Plateau. In the Great Plains and Central Lowland, you roam across miles of grassland. The fall-colored woodlands of the Appalachian Highlands brighten your day before you head down to the beaches of the Coastal Plain. Finally, you hike the Canadian Shield, examining some of the oldest rock exposed on the North American continent, and you stop to see the ice sheet that covers nearly all of Greenland.

From a spacecraft high above earth, you might get a view of North America similar to the one in the painting above. You'd see the physical features—mountains, plains, lakes, and rivers—and the type of ground cover, or what you would find when walking. Bluish white areas show snow or ice. Dark green indicates forested regions. Light green areas are grassland. Brownish yellow shows where deserts lie. Tan areas indicate tundra—the treeless, wide-open areas of the far north.

SUSAN SANFORD

GEOLOGIC REGIONS
OF NORTH AMERICA

WEST COAST (CHAPTER 1)

BASIN AND RANGE
AND MEXICAN HIGHLANDS (CHAPTER 2)

COLORADO PLATEAU (CHAPTER 3)

ROCKY MOUNTAINS
AND COLUMBIA PLATEAU (CHAPTER 4)

GREAT PLAINS
AND CENTRAL LOWLAND (CHAPTER 5)

APPALACHIAN HIGHLANDS
AND COASTAL PLAIN (CHAPTER 6)

CANADIAN SHIELD
AND GREENLAND (CHAPTER 7)

Facing the Coast Of the Pacific

Aboard a boat rocking gently on the surface of Prince William Sound, tourists stare up at a huge wall of ice. The wall is the front end of the Columbia Glacier, one of thousands of ice masses that cover parts of Alaska. Alaska offers the right climate and geography for glacier formation.

A glacier forms where snow falls but never completely melts. As seasons pass, the snow layer grows thicker and heavier. It turns into a thick mass of ice. Eventually the ice begins to move slowly under the pressure of its own weight. Geologists then call it a glacier. It scrapes, crunches, gouges, and reshapes the land it passes over.

Thousands of years ago, during the Ice Age, glaciers ground their way from the Arctic to the middle of North America. They shaped much of the land as you see it today. But glaciers are only one of the forces that change the shape of the land. Powerful movements inside earth also cause changes in the landscape. Where plates of earth's crust come together, they squeeze and bend. This causes faults, or cracks, to form. Pressure in the earth often forces the crust to lift along faults, forming mountains. Magma pushes through the crust and creates volcanoes. Movements of the plates cause earthquakes.

These powerful processes still occur frequently on the West Coast. It's the youngest, most geologically active part of the continent. To explore the rugged West Coast, turn the pages. You'll discover mountains, glaciers, giant trees, a soggy rain forest—and many other wonders.

The Columbia Glacier, a slow-moving river of ice, towers 200 feet (61 m) above Alaska's Prince William Sound. A boat carrying tourists cruises in front of the glacier. The ice advances about 32 feet (10 m) every day. As the glacier moves forward, chunks crack off into the water as icebergs.

Handiwork of Glaciers

Millions of years ago, a block of earth's crust tilted up in what is now California. For thousands of years, streams cut valleys through the block. Later, glaciers—at times almost 4,000 feet (1,219 m) thick—crept into the valleys. The huge tilted block slowly formed the range called the Sierra Nevada, Spanish for "snowy range." Some of these mountains and valleys today are part of Yosemite (yoh-SEM-uh-tee) National Park.

The glaciers came at least three times, deepening and widening Yosemite's valleys each time. When the ice melted, it left behind a spectacular pocket of scenery.

In many places in Yosemite National Park, streams flowing across the park wilderness suddenly reach the edges of steep valley walls. The streams plunge into the valleys, forming numerous scenic waterfalls. One stream drops a total distance of almost half a mile (4/5 km). The plunging water, named Yosemite Falls, is one of the highest waterfalls on earth.

Visitors cool off on Stoneman Bridge, in Yosemite National Park, in California (left). In the background, a peak named Half Dome soars 4,800 feet (1,463 m) above them. Glaciers once carved away part of the mountain. Since then, stone has broken off in thin layers along cracks in the flat face of the granite dome.

The 7-mile-long (11-km) Yosemite Valley (below, at left) lies cradled in the Sierra Nevada range. Grinding glaciers carved the dramatic cliffs and the U-shaped valley less than two million years ago. When the ice retreated, it left behind several valleys branching off the main one. Many waterfalls like the one at right plunge into the valleys.

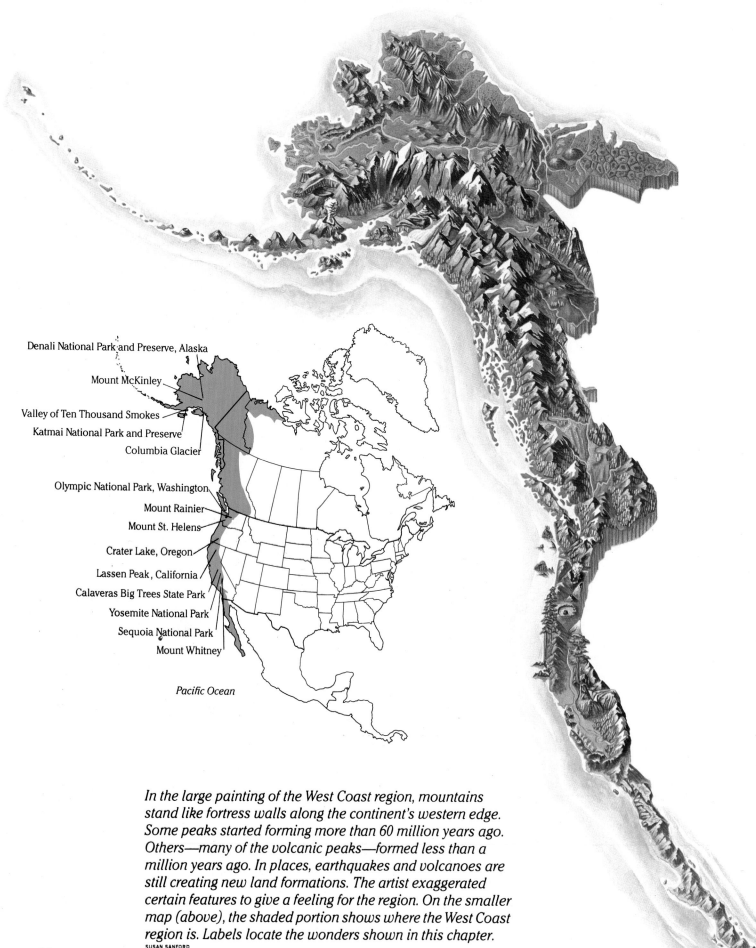

Denali National Park and Preserve, Alaska

Mount McKinley

Valley of Ten Thousand Smokes

Katmai National Park and Preserve

Columbia Glacier

Olympic National Park, Washington

Mount Rainier

Mount St. Helens

Crater Lake, Oregon

Lassen Peak, California

Calaveras Big Trees State Park

Yosemite National Park

Sequoia National Park

Mount Whitney

Pacific Ocean

In the large painting of the West Coast region, mountains stand like fortress walls along the continent's western edge. Some peaks started forming more than 60 million years ago. Others—many of the volcanic peaks—formed less than a million years ago. In places, earthquakes and volcanoes are still creating new land formations. The artist exaggerated certain features to give a feeling for the region. On the smaller map (above), the shaded portion shows where the West Coast region is. Labels locate the wonders shown in this chapter.

SUSAN SANFORD

Sky High

Every year, mountain climbers flock to the eastern edge of Sequoia National Park, in California. They go to explore the rugged landscape around Mount Whitney. The peak, which lies in the Sierra Nevada, was named in 1864 for Josiah Dwight Whitney, the director of California's first geological survey.

A short distance from the mountain, hikers often visit another natural wonder: Tulainyo Lake. At 12,802 feet (3,902 m) above sea level, the lake is the highest in the United States. Its water fills a bowl-shaped formation called a cirque (SERK). An ancient glacier in the region gouged out the cirque, creating the lake when it melted.

Mount Whitney's rocky peak is challenging. But many climbers and hikers reach it every year. One Fourth of July some years ago, a thousand people signed their names in the record book at the top. Today, the National Park Service limits hikers to 50 a day. The regulation helps limit damage to the plants and rocks.

Hikers look across a valley to the jagged top of Mount Whitney, tallest mountain in the lower 48 states. Geologists call the upright rock formations needles. Glaciers carved the smooth lower slopes of the 14,495-foot (4,418-m) mountain. Wind has always blown away enough snow at the summit to prevent the formation of glaciers there.

EUGENE FISHER

Living Giants

Back in 1852, when a hunter named A. T. Dowd first laid eyes on some enormous trees growing in the Sierra Nevada, he raced to tell everyone all about them. The people thought he was telling a tall tale. He wasn't. Anyone who has stood among California's giant sequoias knows that Dowd was not exaggerating.

Two kinds of giant trees grow in California. The climate there provides just the right temperature and moisture for their survival. One kind, the coast redwood, grows near a strip of coast in southern Oregon and northern California. Its wood has a rust-red color. Because the tree lives for centuries, part of its scientific name is *sempervirens*. "Sempervirens" is Latin for "ever-living." The other kind, the giant sequoia, grows only in a narrow stretch of the Sierra Nevada. Like the coast redwood, the giant sequoia lives for centuries. In Calaveras Big Trees State Park, you can see giant sequoias that were already growing at the end of the Roman Empire—about 1,500 years ago.

Giant sequoias (sih-KWOY-uhz) dwarf a visitor at Sequoia National Park (right). The giant sequoia and the coast redwood belong to the same family of trees. Although shown next to each other in the painting below, they don't grow in the same place. The coast redwood, at left, grows near the Pacific coast. The giant sequoia, at right, grows on the western slopes of the Sierra Nevada. Which is larger? The coast redwood is taller. It's the tallest living thing, reaching as high as 350 feet (107 m). But the giant sequoia, also known as the big tree, wins the title of largest living thing on earth. Although the giant sequoia doesn't grow as tall as the redwood, its trunk and branches grow thicker. In total size, it's larger.

© HARALD SUND (RIGHT); GLORIA MARCONI (BELOW)

RICHARD ROWAN

Visitors stand on the Big Stump, what's left of a giant sequoia in California's Calaveras Big Trees State Park (above). People cut the tree down more than 130 years ago. The stump at one time served as a dance floor.

Through the Crust

Inland from the Northwest Coast of the United States lies a band of volcanic peaks. They are part of the Cascade Range. The volcanic mountains formed where one plate of earth's crust slid under the one next to it. Heat inside the earth melted the lower plate, and turned some of that plate into magma. The red-hot magma forced its way to the surface through weak spots in the crust. The eruptions built volcanic mountains.

Some of the Cascade volcanoes are ancient. Oregon's Mount Mazama erupted about 6,600 years ago. Rain and snow filled the hole left behind, creating Crater Lake.

Two volcanoes in the Cascades have erupted during the present century. They poured out lava and filled the sky with ash, steam, and volcanic gases. Lassen Peak blew many times between 1914 and 1921. Mount St. Helens erupted violently as recently as 1980. Geologists cannot say exactly when the next eruption may occur—but they're keeping a close eye on the uneasy Cascades.

Glaciers cap Mount Rainier (ray-NEER), tallest peak in the Cascade Range (left). Mount Rainier, one of several volcanic cones in Washington, was built by the lava, cinders, and ash of repeated volcanic eruptions. Rainier hasn't had a major eruption in 2,000 years. But sometimes it lets off steam through vents near the top. One Cascade volcano, Mount St. Helens, erupted repeatedly in 1980. Ash and gases billow from the peak (below). The ash fell as far away as Maine.

Wizard Island seems to float on the clear blue water of Crater Lake, in Oregon (left). The island is actually one volcanic peak within the remains of another. Long ago, the large mountain, called Mount Mazama, erupted. Its top collapsed inward, forming a wide and deep depression called a caldera (kal-DARE-uh). Rain and melting snow slowly filled the caldera, forming the lake. Later eruptions built up cone-shaped Wizard Island.

A Green Land

When you hear the term "rain forest," do you think of a hot, steamy forest in South America? That's tropical rain forest. Another kind, called temperate rain forest, is cooler, with different kinds of plants. You can find it in Washington, in Olympic National Park.

The park is like three parks in one. It harbors acres of rain forest crowded with ferns, huge trees, and thick mats of hanging moss. It contains jagged young mountains carved by glaciers. And it has a stretch of seacoast battered by violent surf.

About a thousand species, or kinds, of plants grow on Washington's Olympic Peninsula. There are 71 species of moss alone. Roosevelt elk, large members of the deer family, live there. They have been called the gardeners of the rain forest. They eat ferns and other plants, keeping the lower levels of the forest from becoming overgrown.

If you get a chance to visit Olympic National Park, make sure you take rain gear. In parts of the rain forest, about 140 inches (356 cm) of rain falls every year. It may well pour while you're there.

© PAT O'HARA (ABOVE); KEITH GUNNAR/BRUCE COLEMAN INC. (RIGHT)

On a beach in Olympic National Park, in Washington, a starfish called a purple star clings to a rock (above). Tall rock formations called sea stacks jut from the water in the distance. Once part of the Olympic Peninsula, the stacks were isolated offshore by surf pounding away at the land. At right, a visitor marvels at moss-padded trees in the peninsula's rain forest. The thick greenery thrives on the huge amount of rain that falls here every year.

18

White Crown Of the Continent

A massive mountain rises above all its neighbors in Alaska. Glaciers lie near its peaks. Rocky cliffs scar its sides. It's named for William McKinley, the 25th President of the United States. Towering almost four miles (6½ km) above sea level, Mount McKinley remains mostly snow covered throughout the year.

The mountain stands at the edge of Denali National Park and Preserve, an area about the size of Massachusetts. Congress established the park in 1917 to protect the land and the many species of animals there. You can find moose, caribou, Dall sheep, lynx, foxes, wolves, grizzly and black bears, and many kinds of birds in Denali.

Today visitors travel through Denali in shuttle buses—an energy-saving way to get about. The Park Service runs the buses, excluding cars to reduce traffic and pollution. Only visitors with camping permits may drive cars. The system reduced traffic so well that the chances of seeing wildlife have risen. Rangers estimate that you now have a 90 percent chance of seeing animals during a shuttle-bus tour of Denali National Park and Preserve.

That may make up for a frequent frustration that visitors to Denali face—the fact that clouds hide the majestic peak of Mount McKinley about two-thirds of the time.

Visitors gaze at 20,320-foot (6,194-m) Mount McKinley, in Alaska (left). They have traveled in one of the shuttle buses that tour Denali National Park and Preserve. Long ago, Indians named the mountain Denali, *which means "the high one," an appropriate title for North America's tallest peak.*
RICK MCINTYRE/TOM STACK & ASSOCIATES

Full-grown antlers and thick white hair on the neck of a bull caribou (right) are signs of the mating season. Herds of caribou roam widely in Denali National Park and Preserve.

STEVEN C. KAUFMAN

Buried by Nature

In June 1912, in a remote part of south-western Alaska, a volcanic vent near the base of Mount Katmai suddenly burst open. Tons and tons of ash poured out of the new volcano, called Novarupta. It buried many miles of green valley in just a few minutes. The hot ash flow caused streams and underground water to turn to steam. The steam puffed up through openings in the ash called fumaroles.

Four years later, explorers from the National Geographic Society arrived. So many pillars of steam were

still rising from the ash that one man, Robert F. Griggs, named the area the Valley of Ten Thousand Smokes.

This is how Griggs described what he saw: "The whole valley as far as the eye could reach was full of hundreds, no thousands—literally, tens of thousands—of smokes curling from its fissured floor. . . . It was as though all the steam engines in the world, assembled together, had popped their safety valves at once and were letting off surplus steam. . . ."

The area today, reachable only by seaplane or boat, is called Katmai National Park and Preserve. Most of the vents stopped steaming after 50 years, but the enormous wasteland of ash remains. It is a reminder of the most forceful eruption in history to rock North America.

Steam escapes from Trident Volcano (above), one of 12 active volcanoes in Alaska's Katmai National Park and Preserve. Magma inside the volcano produces the steam.

A river in Alaska's Valley of Ten Thousand Smokes erodes, or wears away, a huge layer of ash (left). The ash came from a volcano named Novarupta. The blast, in 1912, buried miles of green valley in drifts of hot ash up to 700 feet (213 m) deep.

Among Ridges And Valleys

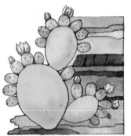

Mono Lake looks fresh and cool under a California sky brushed with clouds. But if you took a drink from it, you wouldn't be refreshed. Like a few other lakes in the region of the Basin and Range and Mexican Highlands, Mono Lake is saltier than the sea. Over time, salt and other minerals from the earth have dissolved and concentrated in the lake.

Mono Lake hasn't always been as salty as it is today. Until 1941, streams from the Sierra Nevada fed the lake. They kept its level up. But as Los Angeles, California, grew, its people needed more water. Engineers routed most of the water from these streams to a large canal system that carries the water to the city. The lake is steadily shrinking. Water evaporates faster than it is replaced. Without the water that once fed it, the lake is becoming saltier. The salt and other minerals become more and more concentrated. Unless some of the streams are allowed to flow back into the lake, the lake eventually will shrink to a fraction of its original size. It will be too salty for the birds and the brine shrimps that live there now.

Changes in Mono Lake caused by humans have been rapid. Forces of nature have acted much more slowly in forming the dry landscapes of the Basin and Range and Mexican Highlands. Starting millions of years ago, long, mountain-size blocks of rock tilted here along cracks in earth's crust. Blocks that tilted up became mountains. Those that tilted down became basins, or valleys. The region is lined with mountain ranges separated by basins.

The waters of Mono Lake (left) mirror pillars of a mineral substance called tufa (TYEW-fuh). For many years, this California lake covered most of the tufa towers. In 1941, water flowing into the lake was rerouted to provide water for Los Angeles, California. The water level in the lake fell, exposing these formations.

Dry, Quiet... And Full of Life

Many people imagine deserts as sandy, lifeless places—and some deserts come close to that. But the Sonoran Desert, in northwestern Mexico and the southwestern United States, is full of life. Creatures and plants have adapted to the dry environment.

People who visit the Sonoran Desert find saguaro cactuses, towering plants with prickly surfaces. Saguaros may live for nearly 200 years. Many don't even grow their armlike branches until they're 50 to 60 years old. Their fruit provides food for birds and other animals.

In the desert, Gila (HEE-luh) woodpeckers nest in holes they dig in cactuses. Speedy roadrunners catch insects and lizards. Slow-moving lizards called Gila monsters rest by day and hunt for food after sundown. Other animals, such as badgers and kangaroo rats, also come out of their burrows at night. Having avoided the heat—and enemies—of the day, they come out in search of food.

If you visit the Sonoran Desert, or other deserts of the Basin and Range and Mexican Highlands, you'll have to look carefully and patiently to find the animals mentioned here. You might not see most of them. They're good at hiding. But you'll know they are there. The desert is not deserted, after all.

At home in the desert, a roadrunner tends its chick in a nest among cactuses (left). Named for its habit of streaking across roads, the bird usually runs instead of flying. It can flee enemies or chase prey on foot at 20 miles an hour (32 km/h).

Saguaro (suh-WAHR-oh) cactuses (right), in the Sonoran Desert in Arizona, may grow as tall as five-story buildings. They spread wide root systems that soak up the little moisture of the desert. The cactuses store water that they use in dry periods.

Great Salt Lake, Utah

Bonneville Salt Flats

Mono Lake, California

Death Valley National Monument

Sonoran Desert

Western Sierra Madre

Huasteca Canyon

Paricutín, Mexico

Horsetail Falls

Eastern Sierra Madre

Like an old-fashioned washboard, much of the Basin and Range and Mexican Highlands region has a rippled surface. Valleys called basins separate about 200 narrow mountain ranges. The artist has drawn only some of the ranges. For millions of years, earth's crust has faulted here. The parts of the crust that tilt upward along the faults create the mountain ranges. Along the coast, to the west, high mountains block most rain clouds moving in from the Pacific Ocean. Very little rain falls in most of the Basin and Range region. Much of the area has become a vast desert. Along the southern edge of the Mexican Highlands, at the bottom of the painting, you see areas where volcanoes occur.

SUSAN SANFORD

A Land Peppered With Salt

An enormous body of water called Lake Bonneville once covered much of western Utah and parts of Idaho and Nevada. Scientists believe that about 15,000 years ago the climate of North America began to grow drier—and Lake Bonneville began to dry up.

Little rain fell, and less and less water flowed into the lake. The lake grew ever smaller. Salt and other minerals in Lake Bonneville became more and more concentrated as the water level dropped, just as in Mono Lake today. Where the lake shrank, it exposed an area crusted with salt—the Bonneville Salt Flats.

Not absolutely every area of Lake Bonneville dried up. Small parts remained, such as Great Salt Lake, in Utah. Great Salt Lake has no outlet. Salt and other minerals continue to dissolve and concentrate in the water. It has become several times saltier than seawater.

A visitor picks up a pinch of salt from the Bonneville Salt Flats, in Utah (below). In ancient times, an immense lake covered the region. Much of the lake dried up. It left behind miles and miles of salt flats—and a few scattered lakes, including Great Salt Lake.

WALTER MEAYERS EDWARDS

Lower Than the Sea

More than a century ago, a small group of travelers searched for a shortcut to the California gold country. A faulty map led them to an intensely hot, dry valley. The group became lost in the valley and wandered for many days with little water. At last they found a tiny spring in the mountains at the edge of the valley. Two of the travelers went off to find food and more water. They returned just in time to save their companions. As the little band finally left, one of them turned around, squinted over the landscape, and said, "Good-bye, Death Valley."

A yearly average of only 1¹/₂ inches (4 cm) of rain falls on Death Valley. In some years, no rain falls. Mountains towering west of the region prevent most rain clouds from reaching the valley. Salt and clay—actually the bottom of an ancient, dried-up lake—cover the center of the dry valley. To the north, sand dunes shift in the hot wind.

The name that the lost traveler gave to this remote place has stuck. Since that time, many other travelers have found that Death Valley is among the hottest and driest places in all of North America.

SEA LEVEL

One spot near Badwater, in California's Death Valley, lies 282 feet (86 m) below sea level. It is the lowest spot on the surface of North America. Miles of land, including mountains, separate the valley from the sea. The painting here shows how low the valley surface would look if you moved it next to the sea. Geologists say Death Valley formed four or five million years ago where earth's crust faulted. Mountain ranges tilted up along the faults. Land between the mountains dropped, creating Death Valley.
GLORIA MARCONI

 DEATH VALLEY

In Death Valley National Monument, a ranger leads hikers toward a lookout point (above). Visitors walking far into the valley should carry plenty of water. Hiking this dry land is thirsty work. In the 1840s, a group of gold seekers found that out when they became lost in the valley. One of those people gave Death Valley its name.

A visitor pauses among lumps of salt on the Devils Golf Course (left). The area was once the bottom of a large, prehistoric lake that has long since dried up. The surface temperature here—one of Death Valley's hottest areas— has reached 190°F (88°C). No wonder Indians gave Death Valley the name Tomesha, *or Ground Afire.*

31

Highland Highlights

A geologist once wrote that on a map of North America, the Basin and Range region looks like "an army of caterpillars crawling northward out of Mexico." Those "caterpillars" are mountain ranges running north and south. You can see them in the painting on page 28. In Mexico, the Sierra Madre ranges lie east and west of a desert-covered plateau called the Mexican Highlands.

Like some areas of the West Coast, the southern boundary of the Mexican Highlands is an active part of earth's surface. Volcanoes rise there in an east-west band across Mexico. In this region, earth's crust has stretched, creating weak areas. Magma pushes up through the weak spots, causing the volcanoes.

At times, major changes have taken place quickly. One

RALPH GATES

Steam and other gases billow from Paricutín (puh-REE-cuh-TEEN), a young volcano in Mexico (above). In 1943, a farmer preparing to plant corn got quite a surprise. Gases started pouring from a vent in his field. The cone of ash and cinders began to grow right before his eyes.

day in 1943, an eruption suddenly occurred in a farmer's field. By the end of the day, ash and cinders had built a good-size mound. After a week, the mound had reached 548 feet (167 m). That's almost as tall as the Washington Monument. Eight months later, the mound had truly become a mountain. It had doubled in height. Today, Paricutín, as the volcanic peak is named, looms 1,345 feet (410 m) above where the farmer's field once lay.

Steep rock walls 1,000 feet (305 m) high catch the evening light in Huasteca (hwas-TEH-ka) Canyon, in northeastern Mexico (above). The canyon lies in a mountain range called the Eastern Sierra Madre. Layers of earth's rocky crust were uplifted here. Then moving water eroded the rock, forming this steep-walled canyon.

From a footbridge near Monterrey, Mexico, a traveler admires a tumbling waterfall (left). Like a horse's tail, the water gracefully falls in a widening pattern. What's the name of this natural wonder? Horsetail Falls!

33

In Waterworn Canyon Lands

When you stand on a rim of the Grand Canyon, in Arizona, a golden eagle may soar *below* you. A mile down, the Colorado River gleams on the canyon floor. Gaze at the colorful stone formations. You are witnessing one of the most remarkable displays of what running water can do.

The Grand Canyon, now a national park, lies in a high, dry region of the continent called the Colorado Plateau. As the Colorado River descends from the Rocky Mountains and winds across the plateau, it picks up tons of silt—tiny rock particles—and acquires its mud-red color. (The word *colorado* is Spanish for "red.") Just as heavy rain carves gullies beside a road, the Colorado River cuts its way into the Colorado Plateau. Geologists say that at the Grand Canyon the process probably began about ten million years ago. It continues as you read this page.

The Grand Canyon doesn't only deepen. It widens, too, as its walls slowly wear away. In places, plant roots grow into cracks in the walls and help break apart the stone. Rain and winter ice also help loosen bits of the exposed rock. Frequent cloudbursts—and gravity—carry the loosened rock downward. In one place, the eroded rims of the Grand Canyon now stand 18 miles (29 km) apart.

The Grand Canyon is only one example of how rain, rushing water, frost, and wind have sculpted a land of layered rock. On the Colorado Plateau, these forces of weathering and erosion have created many natural wonders, some of which you will explore in this chapter.

Massive formations in the Grand Canyon, in Arizona, make tourists on muleback look like toys (left). Geologists believe the Colorado River began carving the mile-deep canyon about ten million years ago. They can read much of the history of the Colorado Plateau in the rock layers exposed on the canyon walls.

WILBUR E. GARRETT, N.G.S. STAFF

Grand-scale Sculpture Gardens

In 1869, geologist John Wesley Powell set out to chart the course of the Colorado River. He followed the river as it flowed through the layered rock of the Colorado Plateau. Powell wrote, "Wherever we look there is but a wilderness of rocks—deep gorges where the rivers are lost below cliffs and towers and pinnacles, and ten thousand strangely carved forms in every direction. . . ."

If you go to Utah, you will see similar kinds of sights, in Bryce Canyon National Park and in Arches National Park, shown on these pages. How did such landscapes form?

Ages ago, movements beneath earth's crust caused vertical cracks called joints to form in the rock layers of the Colorado Plateau. Surface water seeped into the joints. Some of the softer rock fell apart, enlarging the cracks. Water in the cracks froze and expanded, causing the stone to crumble. Rainwater, streams, and melting snow washed away the bits of broken rock. Even today, such weathering and erosion continue to wear away more and more rock. Softer layers wear away faster than harder layers. This leaves behind a variety of stone pinnacles, towers, arches, needles, and other examples of what Powell called "strangely carved forms."

© PETER KRESAN

Water goes to work after a heavy rain in Arches National Park, in Utah (left). Small rocks and particles of clay and sand in the water pour down the canyon wall. The particles help erode the cliff. They scrape off other bits of rock, which the water washes away.

A family hikes along a trail in the Silent City, a section of Bryce Canyon National Park, in Utah (right). Towers of rock rise all around them like skyscrapers. The artists who sculpted these towers? Rain, snow, and ice.
GEORG GERSTER

Monuments to an Age Past

How's this for a long-term project? Start two billion years ago to deposit dozens of layers of sand, of mud, and of lime on earth's surface. The surface at times would be the sea bottom. At other times, when sea level dropped, the surface would be a desert. Let the layers rest on each other for hundreds of millions of years. Allow chemical changes and changes caused by the weight of the layers to turn the layers into rocks of varying hardness. Then let forces within the earth lift the whole area high above sea level. For ten million years, watch streams cut deep, winding canyons. Wait for storms, floods, frost, and wind to whittle away at the layers.

What would you get? The Colorado Plateau.

In simplified terms, that's how the plateau came into being. The sand layers turned into sandstone; the mud into a kind of rock called shale; the lime into limestone.

The rocky shapes in Monument Valley, shown below, are parts of ancient, many-layered deposits of sand. Can you imagine what shapes the forces of nature will create for others to see a million years from now?

Arches National Park, Utah
Canyonlands National Park
Bryce Canyon National Park
Zion National Park
Monument Valley, Arizona and Utah
Grand Canyon National Park, Arizona
Petrified Forest National Park
Four Corners

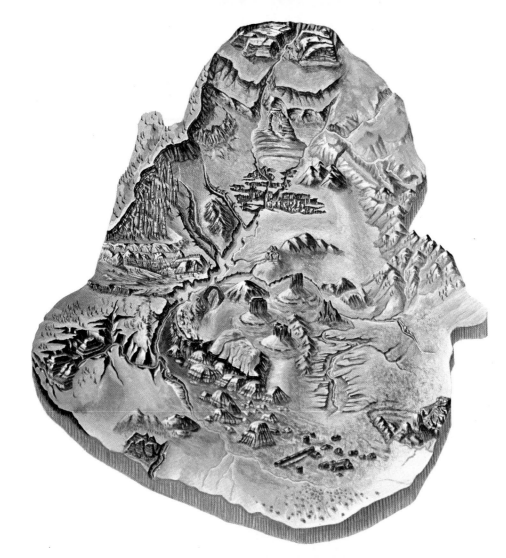

High and dry, the Colorado Plateau is full of fantastic formations shaped by weathering and erosion (left). Here, Colorado, Utah, New Mexico, and Arizona come together at Four Corners—the only place in the U. S. where four states meet (far left). Most of the plateau, a raised landform, lies a mile (1¹/₂ km) above sea level.
SUSAN SANFORD

In Monument Valley, landforms called buttes (BYEWTS) cast long shadows in an Arizona sunset (below). Their flat tops mark the top of a thick layer of sandstone that once covered the area. Water and wind carried away most of the sandstone, leaving the natural monuments. People call the two buttes on the left the Mittens. They'd fit a giant. Each is about 1,000 feet (305 m) tall.

Sands of Time

North of the Grand Canyon, erosion has carved a series of cliffs into "stairs." They are known as the Grand Staircase. Each higher cliff, or stair, exposes younger layers of rock. The sequence of layers from the bottom of the Grand Canyon to the top of the Grand Staircase tells you the geological history of the region.

The name of each cliff—Vermilion, Chocolate, White, Gray, Pink—comes from the color of its rocks.

The canyons of Zion National Park cut into the White Cliffs. The pale sandstone in Zion formed from ancient dunes. A shallow sea spread over the dunes. Dissolved minerals in the seawater seeped into the sand. They cemented the sand into a 2,000-foot-thick (610-m) layer of sandstone. You see some of that pale rock at right.

The top stair, the Pink Cliffs, is youngest and lies farthest from the Grand Canyon. The formations in Utah's Bryce Canyon (pages 36–37) consist of this pink rock.

You can drive to all the stairs in a day. But think—their layers and shapes have taken two billion years to form.

STEPHEN TRIMBLE (BELOW); SAM ABELL (RIGHT)

From Grand View Point, you can see across Monument Basin, in Utah's Canyonlands National Park (above). A dirt road at right reaches about as close to the basin as visitors may travel. No trails descend into the stream-eroded canyons. Riders (right) pause on a steep trail in Zion National Park, also in Utah. You can see layers of sand from ancient dunes in the vertical sandstone wall.

40

Fallen Forest of Stone

In eastern Arizona, hundreds of fallen trees lie scattered about. It looks as if Paul Bunyan had just taken a break from chopping logs. But look more closely. The logs and wood chips in Petrified Forest National Park are all made of multicolored stone.

Indians of this area believed the stone trees were arrow shafts shot by their thunder god. Scientists learned that the stones were once trees. The trees lived in this area about two hundred million years ago. After they fell, they would have rotted quickly on the ground. But they soon became buried in swamps under layers of sand, ash, and mud, called sediments. Through chemical processes, the logs and sediments were slowly changed to stone.

In more recent times, much of the sedimentary rock around the logs has eroded away. The erosion exposed tree fragments made of the hard mineral called quartz.

Some of the logs in Petrified Forest National Park contain gem-quality quartz such as amethyst (AM-uh-thist). People once dynamited the logs, breaking them up to cut, polish, and sell the pieces. President Theodore Roosevelt ended that in 1906. He made the area a national monument. It became a national park in 1962.

Small dinosaurs called Coelophysis *(see-loh-FYE-sis) search for lizards and other prey (below). The painting shows swampy landscape of the Colorado Plateau two hundred million years ago. After trees fell, they were covered by layers of mud, volcanic ash, and sand over a period of millions of years. Today, at Petrified Forest National Park, in Arizona, you can see the petrified remains of those trees.*
GLORIA MARCONI

RICHARD ROWAN (ABOVE); GARY LADD (BELOW)

Broken trunks of ancient trees litter the ground at Petrified Forest National Park (above). What looks like wood is actually stone. Visitors may walk among the logs, but they may not pick up any stones for souvenirs.

Polished petrified wood reveals colors caused by deposits of iron, copper, and other minerals (left). How does wood petrify? Silica, a mineral dissolved in water, seeps into logs buried under sand, ash, and mud. The silica gradually fills and replaces the wood cells, turning the logs into rock-hard quartz.

Across a Mighty Ridge of Stone

Millions of years ago, a shallow sea covered much of western North America. From high ground along the shore, rivers washed mud and sand into the sea. This material settled, forming many layers of sediment. Over a long period of time, the layers hardened into sedimentary rock.

Forces within the earth then began to change the shape of the earth's surface. They pushed up the sedimentary rock beneath the seafloor. Some of the rock was pushed so high that it formed mountains. Material from the seafloor ended up at the top of the Rockies. Streams began to erode the mountains. Glaciers carved them. Forests grew, and animals such as the mountain goat made the mountains their home.

Some parts of the Rockies may have formed when earth's crustal plates pushed against each other. The pressure caused the crust to fold—and to crack in places. You can show with your bedcovers how mountains fold. Smooth the blankets. Then place your hands wide apart on them and slowly push your hands together. Folds and wrinkles like miniature mountain ranges will appear.

Other parts of the Rockies formed when magma forced up portions of earth's crust—just as your toes make bumps in the blankets when you're in bed. Some of the magma broke through the surface. In places, it created volcanoes. In other places, magma flowed out as lava and formed vast pools of melted rock. It hardened, forming the Columbia Plateau, west of the Rockies.

Athabasca Falls fills a gorge with mist in Canada's Jasper National Park. Melting glaciers feed the waterfall. The falls are cutting through layers of sedimentary rock that formed at the bottom of an inland sea ages ago. Sedimentary rock makes up the valleys and many of the mighty peaks of the Rocky Mountains.

GEORG GERSTER

45

A Place of Ancient Ice

Would you like to see what some of North America looked like about 20,000 years ago? Visit the Columbia Icefield, in the Canadian Rockies. This enormous mass of ice includes at least 30 different glaciers. They cover ridges and valleys the way glaciers in the Ice Age covered large areas of North America. Some of the water frozen in the Columbia Icefield may have been there since the Ice Age. You can see remains of this ancient ice gleaming among the mountains in both Banff and Jasper National Parks, in Alberta.

The glaciers reflect the sun so brilliantly that it's often hard to look at them. That's how the region earned its reputation among some North American Indians. They called the icy peaks and ridges the Shining Mountains.

In Banff National Park, most of the glaciers are in valleys so high that only experienced mountain climbers ever set foot on them. But in Jasper National Park, just north of Banff, the Athabasca Glacier has crept down to a spot where anyone can easily reach it.

The Athabasca Glacier looks stationary, but it isn't. It continuously moves downhill. In summer, the lowest tip appears to stop moving downhill because its ice melts faster than the glacier moves. The melting glacier drops gravel, which you can see at left, just beyond the ice.

If you visit the Athabasca Glacier, enjoy it—but watch your step. Deep crevasses, or cracks, cut its icy surface.

With a park guide opposite them, tourists in Jasper National Park peer into a crack called a crevasse (krih-VASS) in the Athabasca Glacier (left). Thousands of crevasses scar the glacier. Some reach down 130 feet (40 m) into the river of ice. Crevasses form when different areas of a glacier move at different speeds. The brittle upper layer of ice cracks open.

Smooth as a mirror, Lake Louise reflects the landscape of Banff National Park in the Canadian Rockies of Alberta (right). Ice Age glaciers advanced and retreated among these mountains, carving steep-sided peaks and U-shaped valleys. Established in 1885 as Canada's first national park, Banff attracts 3 1/2 million visitors a year. It is the most frequently visited national park in Canada.

Backbone of the Continent

When pioneers trudged west across North America, they ran into a barrier. Rearing up out of the plains, the Rocky Mountains seemed to bar the way. Nowadays, you can go by car or by train through the mountains, or fly over them. But the Rockies remain an overwhelming sight however you travel to them.

In the painting on this page, you can see why. The artist exaggerated the features on the map, but not much. The rugged Rocky Mountains *are* a kind of barrier. A boundary called the Continental Divide runs along the highest crests. The Divide separates the directions in which streams and rivers flow from the Rockies. Water to the west of the Divide flows to the Pacific. To the east of the Divide, water eventually drains into the Atlantic Ocean.

SUSAN SANFORD

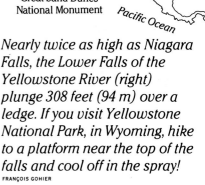

Jasper National Park, Alberta

Columbia Icefield, Alberta and British Columbia

Banff National Park

Waterton–Glacier International Peace Park, Alberta and Montana

Glacier National Park, Montana

Yakima Valley, Washington

Hells Canyon, Idaho and Oregon

Craters of the Moon National Monument, Idaho

Yellowstone National Park, Wyoming

Grand Teton National Park

Capitol Peak, Colorado

Pikes Peak

Great Sand Dunes National Monument

Atlantic Ocean

Pacific Ocean

The massive Rocky Mountains rise in a chain from British Columbia, in Canada, south to New Mexico. Buckling and cracking of earth's crust created some of the ranges. Others rose when magma swelled up below the surface and pushed the crust upward. Huge lava flows bubbling slowly from the earth built the Columbia Plateau, the raised land that extends westward from the rugged spine of North America.

Nearly twice as high as Niagara Falls, the Lower Falls of the Yellowstone River (right) plunge 308 feet (94 m) over a ledge. If you visit Yellowstone National Park, in Wyoming, hike to a platform near the top of the falls and cool off in the spray!

FRANÇOIS GOHIER

Nature's Teakettle

In many parts of North America, you can see old signs of the heat that exists inside the earth. If you visit Craters of the Moon National Monument, in Idaho, you'll see a moonlike landscape of rock. Cone-shaped mounds and craters and open areas of rough black lava lie in every direction. These landforms are the cooled remains of molten, or melted, rock that came up through earth's surface about three million years ago.

In Yellowstone National Park, in Wyoming, heat from the earth reaches the surface of the ground even today. Mud boils in pools. Geysers shoot steam and scalding water into the air. This heat differs from the heat of sand

warmed by the sun. It comes from *inside* the earth. Large reservoirs of superhot magma lie just a few miles below earth's surface at Yellowstone. That's much closer than at most places on earth. Like a burner under a teakettle, the magma heats groundwater that has seeped among the rocks. The heated water surfaces at more than ten thousand hissing and bubbling sites in the park—geysers, hot springs, pools of boiling mud, and steam vents.

PAUL CHESLEY

GEORG GERSTER

Steam billows from Castle Geyser into wintry Wyoming air at Yellowstone National Park (above). Minerals dissolved in the water of the geyser have built up walls around the vent. Behind the trees, Old Faithful also spouts steam. As you might expect, you can count on Old Faithful to erupt regularly—every 33 to 120 minutes.

Cross-country skiers take a dip in Yellowstone National Park (left). A hot spring mixes with the icy stream, making the water lukewarm. Visitors must ask a ranger's permission to swim. Hot springs make swimming dangerous. It's prohibited in most of the park.

Boundary Park

During the summer of 1982, a group of students from the eastern United States used their school vacation to travel west. In Waterton-Glacier International Peace Park, on the United States–Canada border, they hiked rocky trails. Climbing to high points, they enjoyed views of lakes, forests, and towns far below. They examined deep piles of boulders and smaller rocks that glaciers once carried as if they were handfuls of sand.

The park is a kind of open-air geology laboratory. It's an ideal place to examine what glaciers can do. Deep gouges on mountainsides show where rocks that were locked in moving ice scraped across the surfaces. Deposits called moraines—long ridges of rocks, pebbles, sand, and boulders—mark the boundaries where melting glaciers left behind what they had carried.

Back home in Pasadena, Maryland, Matt Melotti recalled his trek to the top of Bear's Hump Trail. The hike took only half an hour. "The experience was a pleasant surprise," Matt says. "It took such little effort to witness an awesome example of a true natural wonder."

Andrew Plotkin, 14, of Pikesville, Maryland, in sunglasses, and Matt Melotti, 13, of Pasadena, Maryland, take a break on Bear's Hump Trail in Waterton-Glacier International Peace Park (below). The park is a monument to the friendship between the U. S. and Canada. Andrew says, "This overlook was the best of our trip west." The boys had a bird's-eye view of Waterton Park, a small Alberta community in the valley below.

Water rushes over a glacier-carved ledge in Glacier National Park, in Montana (above). As it melted, the glacier dropped boulders in its path. Some 60 glaciers dot the mountains of this park, just south of the border between the United States and Canada.

An ancient fault splits Bearhat Mountain, in Glacier National Park, in Montana (left). Hidden Lake sparkles beneath, in a depression dug by a vanished glacier. A mixture of rain and melting snow and ice provides the lake water.

Jagged Giants of Wyoming

Grand Teton National Park, in Wyoming, lies along a fault in earth's crust. Ages ago, tension in the crust caused the land on each side of the fault to move. One side sank, creating the valley called Jackson Hole. The other side tilted, forming the towering Tetons. Ice Age glaciers carved the peaks into the jagged shapes you see below. By a geologist's standards, the Tetons are young. They began to rise about 9 million years ago. Most of the Rockies are 40 million to 65 million years old.

The Tetons—and other ranges in the Rockies—are home to a wide variety of wildlife, including bears, moose, and elk. The elk find plenty of food in high mountain meadows in summer. But in winter, heavy snows force them down into valleys in search of food.

Part of the largest elk herd on the continent spends the winter in Jackson Hole. Today, farms and ranches have taken up most of the valley. The animals cannot find enough to eat on their own to last the winter. To help them, the government has set aside land in the National Elk Refuge. There, the U. S. Fish and Wildlife Service provides food in winter. When spring arrives, the elk leave the refuge and return to the mountain meadows.

The Teton Range soars above a broad Wyoming valley called Jackson Hole (below). Glaciers carved the jagged peaks after part of earth's crust tilted and was forced sky high along a fault. Erosion has barely had a chance to smooth the nine-million-year-old giants. At right, two bull elk practice facing off with their antlers in a test of strength. About 7,500 elk spend the winter in the National Elk Refuge, at the foot of the Tetons in Jackson Hole.

Colorado Climbers

A woman named Katharine Lee Bates stood at the top of Pikes Peak in 1893 and looked at the mountains around her. What she saw of the Colorado Rockies inspired her to write a poem about "purple mountain majesties." The poem, with music added, became a familiar song. It's called "America the Beautiful."

The mountain ranges around Pikes Peak aren't really purple—unless they're painted that color by a spectacular sunset. But they are majestic. Colorado contains the tallest peak of all the Rocky Mountains: Mount Elbert, which rises to an elevation of 14,433 feet (4,399 m).

The Colorado Rockies provide exciting challenges to a great many hikers and climbers. Yet in the mid-1800s, people who were neither hikers nor climbers flocked to the mountains. What attracted them? Gold and silver. The precious metals had been discovered in the Colorado Rockies, and a stampede had begun. Determined prospectors on their way to the Rocky Mountains adopted as their motto, "Pikes Peak or Bust!"

Pikes Peak was named for Zebulon Pike, an army officer and explorer who led an expedition into the Rockies in 1806. Tired troops, inadequate supplies, and bad weather prevented Pike from climbing to the summit. Today, you can reach the top by foot, by car, or by train.

Early sunlight bathes snowy Pikes Peak, in Colorado, during an Easter service (left). The 14,110-foot (4,301-m) peak is among the first that travelers spot while traveling west across the Great Plains.

Mountaineering students search for footholds on Capitol Peak, in Colorado (right). Climbers have nicknamed this area Knife-edge Ridge. More than 50 peaks in the Colorado Rockies rise higher than 14,000 feet (4,267 m). This treacherous ridge makes Capitol Peak one of the hardest "fourteeners" to climb.

Built by the Wind

Great Sand Dunes National Monument looks like a sandbox for a giant's children. The hills of shifting sand are the tallest dunes in North America—and they're nowhere near a seashore. They lie in a valley in Colorado, at the foot of the Sangre de Cristo Mountains.

How did the sand get there? Winds have been depositing it at the foot of the mountains for thousands of years. The winds pick up the sand from the dry San Luis Valley nearby and carry it along. As the winds approach the wall created by the Sangre de Cristo Mountains, they slow down and deposit the sand.

Scientists think that if all the sand in the dunes could be cemented together, it would form a cube with sides 8 miles (13 km) in length. If you visit the giant sandbox, you may scramble up, tramp around, and slide down the dunes. It's best to visit early in the morning or near sunset. The sand is cooler then, and dramatic shadows spread across the landscape. You might find yourself imagining that you're in the Sahara, in Africa.

A thunderstorm draws a curtain of rain over Great Sand Dunes National Monument, in Colorado. For centuries, wind steadily sweeping sand from the southwest has built the drifting dunes.
© PAT O'HARA

"YOU'RE 7,900 FEET DOWN ALMOST A HALF MILE DEEPER THAN THE GRAND CANYON!"

"WOW!"

The ledges of Hells Canyon, between Idaho and Oregon, drop 7,900 feet (2,408 m) to the deep and narrow Snake River (above). Millions of years ago, lava poured out of cracks in the earth's crust. The molten material hardened into a rock called basalt (buh-SAWLT). Since then, the Snake River has carved down through the rock layers, creating the world's deepest gorge.
GLORIA MARCONI

Cliffs in Hells Canyon tower above boaters and rafters on the Snake River (left). The canyon forms part of the Idaho-Oregon border. In the course of its 100-mile (161-km) journey through Hells Canyon, the winding Snake River crashes through some of North America's most exciting rapids.
GEORG GERSTER

Land of Lava

You've scaled the Rockies. Now travel down their western slopes onto the Columbia Plateau. At this point in your trip through North America's wonders, you may think there's little left that could impress you.

But then you reach western Idaho and arrive at Hells Canyon, the deepest gorge in the world. The Snake River has cut far down into the basalt of the Columbia Plateau, exposing huge cliffs of the black and gray volcanic rock.

The basalt formations in Hells Canyon and elsewhere on the Columbia Plateau are hardened lava. Over and over again, molten rock oozed from hundreds of cracks in earth's crust. The lava spread across the land, cooling into a thick, rocky covering. This covering of ancient lava blankets an area about twice the size of New York State. If you visit the Columbia Plateau, where Idaho, Oregon, and Washington come together, you'll stand on the largest area of volcanic rock in North America.

Wheat grows on a high ridge above the patchwork fields of Yakima Valley, in Washington (below). Fertile soil in the region covers thick beds of lava, now hardened, that flowed out of the earth over millions of years. Volcanic ash enriches the soil. Irrigation provides plenty of water. And the sun shines most days of the year. Some Yakima Valley fields yield twice as much produce as farms the same size in other parts of North America.

In the Heart Of the Continent

When pioneers set out from the East during the past century, they spent weeks rolling in wagons across seemingly endless plains. Those who took a route called the Oregon Trail whooped with joy when they spotted a tall rock formation (left). They knew from earlier travelers that this landmark indicated progress across the Great Plains. Many wrote in their diaries about sighting Chimney Rock.

The trip across the grasslands of the continent's interior was—and is—a long journey. The area contains one-quarter of all the land in North America.

The soil of the Great Plains was formed largely from sediment washed from the Rocky Mountains. The plains start at the foot of the Rockies. Grasses blanket much of the plains—except where farms cover them with grain. In much of the region, ranches and farms have replaced the grasslands where bison, or buffalo, once roamed.

The plains roll eastward into the Central Lowland. This area, twice as large as Texas, consists of gently rolling land that huge ice sheets helped shape thousands of years ago. The Great Lakes border the region to the north, the Appalachian Mountains to the east.

If you travel across the Great Plains and Central Lowland, you'll spend periods of time on straight roads that stretch ahead as far as you can see. Perhaps you'll be the first person in the car to spot the next town or one of the landmarks that excited the early settlers. Keep your eyes open. There are many wonders to be seen in the region.

Chimney Rock stands on the plains of western Nebraska under a summer thunderstorm (left). You can drive past the formation today on Nebraska 92, a highway that runs near the Oregon Trail here. Settlers traveled the old trail a century ago. Many left their names carved in the clay-and-sandstone tower.

DAVID HISER/ASPEN

The Badlands

Sharp ridges cut into the sky. Canyons and gullies hide pyramids, knobs, and strangely shaped rock columns called hoodoos. Some Sioux (SOO) Indians called this landscape *makosche shicha,* or "bad land." French trappers referred to the hot, rugged area as *les mauvaises terres à traverser,* or "bad lands to cross."

Badlands form as rain and streams carve deep into layers of sandstone and hardened mud. With every rain, the badlands change a bit more. You can visit this kind of landscape in Badlands National Park, in South Dakota, and in Canada's Dinosaur Provincial Park, in Alberta.

The two parks hold some of the richest sources of fossils anywhere. Scientists—and erosion—have uncovered hundreds of dinosaur skeletons in the Canadian park. From fossils found in the U. S. park, scientists have learned that camels, three-toed horses, and saber-toothed cats lived there 35 million years ago.

PAUL VON BAICH (BELOW); JIM BRANDENBURG (RIGHT)

Fossil specialist Darren Tanke describes a horned dinosaur at Dinosaur Provincial Park, in Alberta (above). Part of the fossil skull of the dinosaur lies uncovered in sandstone. In South Dakota, the rough landscape of Badlands National Park (right) ends suddenly where it meets the plains. Streams and rain have been carving these ridges and valleys in the layered stone for thousands of years—and the process continues today.

Dinosaur Provincial Park, Alberta

Devils Tower National Monument, Wyoming

Badlands National Park, South Dakota

Chimney Rock, Nebraska

Carlsbad Caverns National Park, New Mexico

Chicago, Illinois

Lake Superior

Lake Ontario

Niagara Falls

Lake Erie

Lake Huron

Lake Michigan

Mammoth Cave National Park, Kentucky

Before settlers came, prairie grasses covered millions of acres in the Great Plains and Central Lowland region (right). Today, if you fly over the area, ranches and squared-off farm fields make the central part of North America look like a patchwork quilt. The Great Plains begin at the foot of the Rockies and spread eastward, rolling into the Central Lowland. The western part of the region, shielded by the Rockies, receives less windblown moisture than eastern areas. As a result, western grasses are shorter than those to the east.

SUSAN SANFORD

66

Skyscrapers and Ground Scrapers

From the city of Chicago, Illinois, Lake Michigan looks more like an ocean than like a lake. On a windy day, you can stand on one of the city's wide beaches and see breakers rolling ashore. Huge tankers cruise along in the distance. The water—fresh rather than salt—stretches all the way to the horizon.

How did this long and broad lake form? During the Ice Age, thick glaciers gouged their way down from the north. They scooped out weak rock, forming the basins that now hold Lake Michigan and the other four Great Lakes. The others—Superior, Huron, Erie, and Ontario—lie on the border between the United States and Canada.

Eventually, the huge sheets of ice began to melt as the earth's climate grew warmer. Meltwater from the glaciers helped fill the basins, forming the Great Lakes.

Chicago, Illinois, built by human hands, overlooks Lake Michigan (below), built ages ago by the gouging action of glaciers. Cracked, wind-streaked ice glazes the surface of the lake in winter.

Grass as Far As the Eye Can See

"There was nothing but land," says a character in Willa Cather's novel *My Ántonia*, a book about people on the Great Plains. There was land and tall grass... and more grass. Few features stood as landmarks. In places, early settlers going west drove stakes into the ground as signposts for others to follow.

A hundred years ago, grasses covered much more territory than they do today. The land supported many kinds of animal life, especially bison. When pioneers first headed west, they saw bison herds so large that it was impossible to count the animals. People measured the herds in miles. In the 1860s, for example, a soldier reported seeing a herd of bison in Kansas some 60 miles long and 20 miles wide (97 by 32 km). People killed many bison for their hides and meat, or simply for sport. Eventually, ranchers took over land. And farmers known as sodbusters turned up the tough grasses with plows. They made farms out of the bison grazing grounds. Today, far fewer bison remain—but these hump-shouldered beasts have made a comeback in several protected areas.

NICHOLAS DE VORE III/BRUCE COLEMAN INC. (LEFT); JIM BRANDENBURG (BELOW)

On a grassy Montana hillside (left), a farmer with his team of workhorses surveys a field of cut-and-baled alfalfa. Before the arrival of settlers, bison by the million roamed free on great areas of grass such as this. Above, wild flowers called blazing stars cover a prairie in Iowa.

Heart of a Volcano

Among the grasslands and low hills of an area in northeastern Wyoming, Devils Tower is the tallest thing in sight. Indians who once spent winters nearby told legends about the tower. One story describes how a giant bear made grooves in the tower by dragging its claws down the rock. Those "bear scratches" are columns of rock that formed when molten volcanic rock cooled. The cooling rock cracked into multisided columns that stand exposed in vertical patterns.

Devils Tower attracts more than a thousand climbers a year. The first known to reach the top got there in 1893. He used a ladder hung from pegs driven into the rock. In 1941, a stuntman took another route. He parachuted from a plane. Once on top, he couldn't get down. Pilots dropped him food, which he shared with the small animals that live on top of the tower. After six days, trained mountaineers climbed the tower and rescued him.

How did Devils Tower form? ***1.*** *Ages ago, a volcano erupted (below) in what is now the state of Wyoming. Continued eruptions of cinders and ash gradually built a cone-shaped mountain. After the final eruption of the volcano, the magma in the core cooled. It hardened into a plug of rock.* ***2.*** *For millions of years, the ash and cinders of the cone eroded away from the more resistant core.* ***3.*** *All that remains of the volcano today is the projecting plug. Geologists call it a volcanic neck.*

No, it's not a giant tree stump (below). It's Devils Tower, a tall rock formation in Wyoming. In 1906, President Theodore Roosevelt declared it a national monument, the first in the United States. Long ago, some Indians believed that an evil spirit lived in the tower. They called it The Bad God's Tower. The old legend hasn't kept rock climbers away. Three of them (right) work their way up the 865-foot-high (264-m) face of the tower.

STEVEN C. WILSON/ENTHEOS (ABOVE); GLORIA MARCONI (BELOW); MARK NEWMAN/EARTH IMAGES (OPPOSITE)

1

2

3

Inside the Crust

Lines of people wind down paths—down, and down, and down. Electric lights installed by the National Park Service take the place of daylight. If you join these lines, you'll walk *inside* the continent—in Carlsbad Caverns National Park, in New Mexico, and in Mammoth Cave National Park, in Kentucky. So far, on your tour of the natural wonders of North America, you've seen many surface landforms carved by water. In these two parks, you'll see wonders that water creates underground.

How does water begin to carve a cave? Rainwater combines with carbon dioxide from the air. This forms a weak acid that seeps down through cracks in limestone underground. Dissolving the rock, the acidic groundwater opens up spaces that slowly grow larger.

You might think that dark caverns don't support life, but they do. Thousands of bats live in Carlsbad during part of the year. It was the nightly flight of bats leaving the cave that led people to it in the first place. In Mammoth Cave, crayfish and blind, colorless fish live in underground streams.

DAVID HISER/ASPEN

Visitors view mysterious shapes in New Cave (left). It's one of 71 known caves in Carlsbad Caverns National Park, in New Mexico. The shapes form as water containing dissolved limestone drips from the ceiling, leaving mineral deposits on the ceiling and floor. The networks of caves at Carlsbad began to form when acidic groundwater seeped through limestone and slowly dissolved the rock.

Visitors study the domed ceiling of Chief City, an underground room in Mammoth Cave National Park, in Kentucky (right). Mammoth is the world's longest known cave system.
CHIP CLARK

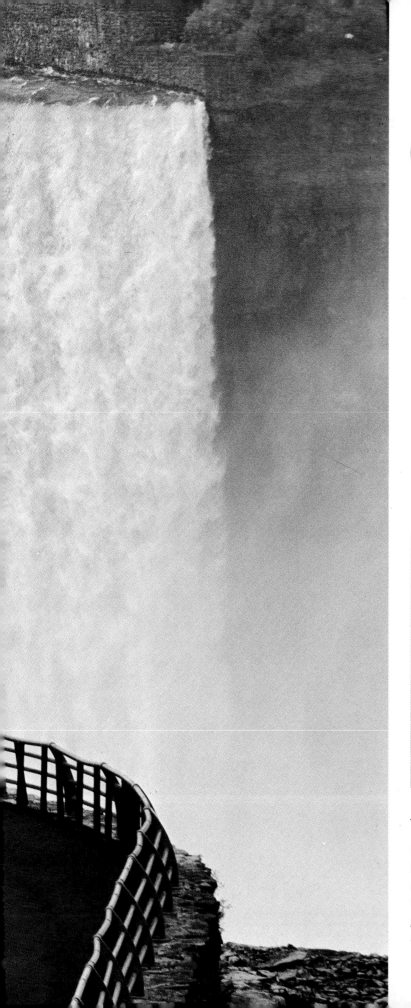

Crashing Waters

The Niagara River flows gently out of Lake Erie. Then it heads for a dramatic change. After dropping over Niagara Falls, it leaps and roars through Niagara Gorge, where it swirls violently in a large whirlpool.

Unlike many waterfalls, Niagara drops straight. The rock ledge at the top of the falls is harder than rock below it. As the softer rock erodes from under the ledge, the river spills over the ledge like water poured from a pitcher.

Niagara Falls developed at the end of the Ice Age as enormous ice sheets melted. Water from the new Lake Erie flowed to a cliff at the edge of Lake Ontario. Pouring over the cliff, the water formed Niagara Falls. As the water eroded soft rock under the cliff, pieces of the harder cliff edge occasionally broke off. This has continued to happen ever since. The falls have moved slowly upstream. Geologists say the falls have eroded their way some 7 miles (11 km) upstream since forming about 12,000 years ago.

CRAIG AURNESS/WEST LIGHT (LEFT); © BARRIE ROKEACH 1984 (BELOW)

A rainbow arches in the mist above Horseshoe Falls (above), part of Niagara Falls. From Terrapin Point on Goat Island, in the middle of the Niagara River, visitors watch as the river tumbles into a gorge (left). Goat Island divides the Niagara River. It sends 90 percent of the river over Horseshoe Falls, on the Canadian side, and 10 percent over the American Falls, on the United States side. Goat Island is part of New York State.

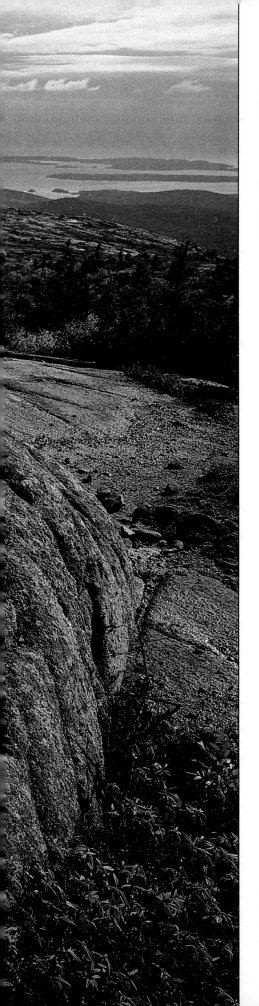

6 Approaching The Atlantic

From an airplane, Mount Desert Island, off the coast of Maine, looks like a giant lobster claw laid out on the blue water. The island's granite mountaintops merge into spruce-covered hills where white-tailed deer nibble plants and squirrels play. At the edge of the island, cliffs meet the sea.

If you visit Mount Desert Island, you may decide to hike to the top of Cadillac Mountain, in Acadia National Park. At 1,530 feet (466 m), Cadillac is the tallest peak on the Atlantic coast of the United States. During winter, it's one of the first spots in the U. S. to be touched by the rising sun. From the top, you can see the ocean all around you.

Millions of years ago, this same mountain was part of the mainland. The ocean was farther to the east. During the Ice Age, glaciers covered this part of the continent. At one time, Cadillac Mountain lay under ice about a mile (1½ km) thick. The weight of the ice pushed down the land. The movement of the ice widened and deepened valleys. As the climate warmed up, the glaciers began to melt. The land started to bounce back up again. But sea level was also rising as meltwater flowed into the ocean. Flooded valleys became bays. Mountains and hills became coastal islands like Mount Desert Island.

You'll visit other islands, too—islands untouched by Ice Age glaciers. (Along the coast, the glaciers reached only as far south as present-day New York City.) These islands, called barrier islands because they stretch like barricades off the coast, look very unlike Mount Desert.

Rounded granite and scattered evergreens top Cadillac Mountain, in Acadia National Park, in Maine (left). The Atlantic Ocean lies in the distance. The crisscross grooves in the granite were once only cracks. Thousands of years of rain, and freezing and thawing, have turned the cracks into deep scars.
© DAVID MUENCH

The Color of Fall

When settlers arrived in North America, they found vast stretches of forested countryside. Much of what grew was broadleaf forest, mostly made up of trees that lose their leaves every year after they change color. The wood of many kinds of broadleaf trees, such as maples and oaks, is popular for making furniture.

As demand increased, people cut more and more of these trees. They also used other kinds of trees, such as fir and pine, for construction. Much of the forest eventually gave way to farms, villages, cities, and roads.

Nevertheless, some forests survived. Others, cut at one time, have been allowed to grow back again. Today, many wooded areas are protected. They shelter animals and plants and provide people with a sample of the woods their ancestors knew. From Newfoundland to Alabama, along the wooded slopes of the Appalachian Mountains, you can enjoy shady forests and fall colors that long ago greeted Indians and early settlers.

N.G.S. PHOTOGRAPHER DAVID ALAN HARVEY (BELOW); DAVID CUPP (RIGHT)

Fall-colored forest blankets Great Smoky Mountains National Park (above). The park preserves some of the oldest, most varied broadleaf forest in North America. (Most broadleaf trees shed their leaves in autumn.)

Scarlet maples and golden birches reflect in a stream in New Hampshire's White Mountain National Forest (right). Chemical action in leaves causes them to change color as fall arrives. Visitors flock to the woods of the East to enjoy the brilliant displays of autumn.

Atlantic Ocean

Bay of Fundy, Canada
Cadillac Mountain,
Acadia National Park, Maine
Mount Washington, New Hampshire
White Mountain National Forest
Cape Hatteras, North Carolina
Outer Banks
Great Smoky Mountains
National Park,
Tennessee and North Carolina
Lake Okeechobee, Florida
Everglades National Park

Mississippi
River

Gulf of Mexico

The Appalachians, among the oldest mountains in North America, stretch from Newfoundland to Alabama. The mountains formed when earth's crust, under pressure, was folded into long ridges with valleys in between. During the Ice Age, glaciers rounded off peaks and gouged out lakes in the northern Appalachians. Rain and frost have worn down the southern mountains, which were untouched by glaciers. Rivers carry sand, clay, and bits of rock toward the Atlantic Ocean and the Gulf of Mexico. As the rivers deposit this material, they build a broad plain along the coast.

SUSAN SANFORD

Weather-beaten Peak

GLORIA MARCONI

A foggy wind often blows at the summit of Mount Washington in winter. The fog coats everything with a layer of ice—including the weather station atop the 6,288-foot-high (1,917-m) peak. The instruments at the weather station have measured some of the world's worst weather. The fastest gust of wind recorded anywhere on earth blew there in April 1934. It roared across the summit at 231 miles an hour (372 km/h), more than three times as fast as hurricane winds. If the buildings on the mountain hadn't been held down with heavy chains anchored in solid rock, they might have blown away.

You can hike, drive, or ride a cog railway up Mount Washington in the warmer months. Even then you might find harsh weather. Snow has fallen in July. Records show 100-mile-an-hour (161-km/h) winds in all months.

Snowy Mount Washington, in New Hampshire (below), lies in the path of heavy storms that batter the East Coast. Winter weather is so severe that a weatherman at the peak (above) must tend outdoor instruments every 45 minutes. A coating of ice called rime has to be chipped off the instruments so they will work. Even in summer, hikers must be prepared for fog, cold rain—and snow.

The Ups and Downs Of a Canadian Bay

You wake up on your first morning at the upper shores of the Bay of Fundy. You look out your window. Mud! Why, you wonder, do they call these mud flats between Nova Scotia and New Brunswick a bay? If you look again about six hours later, you'll see why. These Canadian mud flats will be covered by water.

What happened to the area where birds gathered clams and sea worms just hours before? The answer: The tide came in. Tides in the Bay of Fundy vary more between low and high tide than any other tides in the world.

The Micmac Indians who lived in this part of Canada

At low tide, boats lie aground at Hantsport Wharf, near the Bay of Fundy in Nova Scotia (above). The owners of these Canadian vessels don't worry about getting their boats afloat. The incoming tide will take care of that.

explained the tides in a legend. They said that a giant once sat down here to take a bath. When he stood up, the water sloshed back and forth, starting the big tides.

Actually, it is the shape of the Bay of Fundy that causes the huge tides. The bay is somewhat funnel shaped. Wide at its mouth, it gets narrower and shallower toward its upper end. When the Atlantic Ocean tide comes in, a vast amount of water rushes into the mouth of the bay. As the rising water funnels in, the narrowing shores of the bay force the water level up. The water rises dramatically for six hours. Then it drops again as the tide goes out.

Mud flats appear as the tide goes out in the upper Bay of Fundy (below). For six hours at low tide, gulls, sandpipers, and other shorebirds take advantage of exposed mud. They swoop or scurry about, picking up clams and sea worms.

As the tide comes in (above), the boats shown at far left float on plenty of water. Tidal variation in the Bay of Fundy is the greatest in the world. At the narrow end of the bay, the highest tides rise 53 feet (16 m).

83

M-I-S-S-I-S-S-I-P-P-I

The Mississippi: Always fun to spell, this long and powerful river is one of the greatest shipping channels in the world. The captains of many kinds of ships depend on the river to move their freight.

Would you believe that you can wade across the river? You can...if you travel upriver as far as Lake Itasca. From the edge of that clear lake in Minnesota, the Mississippi begins its long trip as a mere trickling stream.

Chippewa (CHIP-uh-wah) Indians gave the river its name. They called it *Messipi*, or Great River. On its winding 2,348-mile (3,779-km) journey to the Gulf of Mexico, the Mississippi is joined by thousands of other streams. Eventually, the river provides an escape route for the waters of almost half of the United States—including all or part of thirty-one states—and two Canadian provinces.

About halfway along the route of the Mississippi, the muddy Missouri River flows in from the west. It turns the Mississippi the color of milky coffee. At Cairo (CAY-roe), Illinois, the Ohio River joins the Mississippi. Over the remaining 1,200 miles (1,931 km), the broad river winds and loops its way to the Gulf of Mexico.

The Mississippi has often shifted its course. The original site of Kaskaskia, Illinois, today lies buried in mud under the river. The Mississippi has also flooded fields and farms. Now engineers help control the river with dams and flood channels. They build up banks called levees (LEV-eez), too. Except in the worst floods, these projects help hold the river between its banks.

Modern-day Huck Finns and Tom Sawyers bait their fishhooks at the edge of the Mississippi River (left). The scene would have looked familiar to Mark Twain. He wrote several books about life on the mighty river near which he spent his boyhood.

Sunrise glistens on the wide river as a towboat pushes heavily loaded barges toward Greenville, Mississippi (below). Barge fleets carry oil, grain, coal, and other products up and down the Mississippi. The Mississippi is part of the fourth longest river system in the world.

A Land of Water

To the Seminole Indians, the low-lying wetlands called the Everglades are known as the "grassy waters." These waters cover most of the southern tip of Florida and lie largely within Everglades National Park. About 300 kinds of birds live there. Alligators swim in inland waterways, along with turtles, snakes, otters, and fish. Sawgrass covers huge areas. Groups of cypress trees shelter marsh rabbits, deer, bears, and other animals. Clumps of mangrove trees form a seaside maze.

The Everglades formed because of the natural flooding of Lake Okeechobee. Floods created a system of shallow waterways throughout the area. Periods of high water alternated with dry periods. The cycle of wet and dry provided a perfect habitat for a variety of plants and animals.

People now use floodgates and canals to control the level of Lake Okeechobee. The water is regulated for farms, houses, and industry. People's needs can upset the natural cycle of wet and dry in the swamp. Scientists are watching to see how human control of the water affects the plants and animals of the Everglades.

GEORG GERSTER (BELOW); FRANÇOIS GOHIER/ARDEA LONDON (RIGHT)

Thick sawgrass and floating water lilies grow in Florida's Everglades National Park (above). Visitors survey the watery world from an observation platform.

Like scattered pieces of a jigsaw puzzle, the Ten Thousand Islands spread along the Gulf coast of the Everglades (right). Mangrove trees help form the islands. Their roots trap dead leaves that decay, creating soil.

In shallow water, an alligator waits for prey in the Everglades sun (above). A great egret lands at the swamp (below). The alligator and the egret were once endangered. People hunted the alligator for its hide, and the egret for its showy feathers. Today, laws protect both animals. Alligators, egrets, and many other creatures thrive in the marshes and waterways of Everglades National Park.

Where Surf Pounds the Sandy Edge

The process of erosion gradually changes every landscape on earth's surface. But in most places, the change is so slow that you don't notice it happening. If you return to the same mountainside camp in New Hampshire every year, you can depend on seeing familiar trails to guide you on your hikes.

That's not true on the Outer Banks. These are narrow barrier islands off the coast of North Carolina. Visit the Outer Banks one summer. Return the next summer and you may find that surf has washed away the beach trail—or the beach—where you had walked the previous year.

The Outer Banks are islands made of sand. When Ice Age glaciers melted, the sea level rose. Most geologists believe that waves then pushed sand from the seafloor to shore. There the sand piled up in long ridges. Wind blew the sand higher into dunes. Storm waves cut through the dunes in places, and the sea surrounded them. In this way, the dunes became islands—the Outer Banks.

Almost as temporary as a sandcastle built on the edge of the sea, a barrier island beach may change shape in a day, or in just an hour, if a strong storm moves in. And always the waves pound, and pound, and pound.

N.G.S PHOTOGRAPHER DAVID ALAN HARVEY (BOTH)

Since 1870, the Cape Hatteras Lighthouse (left), in North Carolina, has warned sailors of danger. Today, the lighthouse itself is in danger. Only a narrow strip of sand separates the lighthouse from the pounding sea.

Wave after wave roars ashore under a pier at Nags Head, on North Carolina's Outer Banks (above). Wind, tides, and stormy surf continuously reshape the sandy barrier islands that lie along the Atlantic coast.

North to a Land Both Old and Cold

In the northernmost parts of the continent, the land lies frozen and quiet for much of the year. An occasional polar bear trudges across the empty landscape, but most of the time the scene remains deserted and still. With the arrival of the sunny days of summer, however, the North changes.

The area is full of life in summer. Hundreds of kinds of plants bloom. Insects buzz. Small rodents called lemmings scurry about, searching for food. Many kinds of birds nest there. Caribou herds graze.

The treeless plain where all this happens is called tundra. The tundra covers huge areas around the northern parts of Hudson Bay, in Canada. It reaches high into the Arctic on the northern islands. On much of the tundra, hummocks—rounded clumps of soil and plants—stretch as far as you can see. Bare rock sticks through in spots.

Summer in the Arctic lasts only two months or so. But during that time, the sun shines almost 24 hours a day. Snow on the ground melts, and the surface soil thaws. Less than a yard (1 m) down, however, the ground stays frozen. Rain and melted snow have nowhere to drain, so pools, puddles, and lakes of all sizes appear everywhere. They create perfect breeding places for mosquitoes, blackflies, and other biting insects.

People have called these insects "the plague of the tundra." Insects by the billion buzz during the summer. Anyone out on the tundra slaps at them all day long—and listens to them hovering about the tent at night.

Low-growing tundra plants carpet a slope (left) on Canada's Bylot Island, in the Arctic. Tundra is the term for the treeless plains of the far north. Walking on tundra in summer is tiring. Tough clumps of plants tilt when you step on them. Then your feet slip into the spongy ground between the clumps. It's slow going!

Icy Architecture

In an igloo made of snow blocks, two fishermen take shelter from the freezing wind. The two Inuit (IN-oo-it), or Eskimos, are camping near a lake west of Hudson Bay, in northern Canada. Although it is already spring, they still had to chop a fishing hole through ice about 4 feet (1¼ m) thick.

Today, most of the 17,000 Inuit west of Hudson Bay live in villages. They build igloos for shelter only when they hunt or fish in the wilderness.

The Inuit and their ancestors have fished and hunted this region for a thousand years. Frozen from fall to spring, their home is known as the Barren Grounds. To people accustomed to lawns and trees, the area might seem barren, or empty. No trees grow here. For much of the year, the cold is so bitter it can freeze human skin in 30 seconds. But to the Inuit, it is home.

Does the region look hard to live in today? Twenty thousand years ago, it would have been impossible to live there. The area was being squashed by the thickest ice of the Ice Age. The ice lay in the area of Hudson Bay. Its heavy weight created the depression the bay fills today.

Ancient rock almost two billion years old lies exposed on Marble Island, in Canada's Hudson Bay (right). Inuit, or Eskimos, tell a legend that the uninhabited island is an iceberg turned to stone.

The Canadian Shield, with Hudson Bay at the center, covers about a quarter of the continent. Although trees grow in the south, tundra covers most of the north. Lakes and streams lie everywhere. For hundreds of thousands of years, sheets of ice up to 2 miles (3 km) thick covered the land. The moving ice leveled several mountain chains and exposed some of earth's oldest rocks. Areas in gray are not part of the shield.

SUSAN SANFORD

Polygons and Pingos

Parts of North America are so cold that beneath the surface the ground stays frozen permanently. This condition is called permafrost. In summer, permafrost keeps melted snow from seeping much below the surface of the ground. Many pools form. Where they don't, permafrost at least keeps the tundra soggy. By preventing water from soaking in, permafrost also helps form special tundra features called pingos and polygons.

A pingo is a hill that forms where a lake has filled up with dirt. Water that collects under the dirt is trapped between permafrost below and loose soil above. As the water freezes, it expands, as does all water turning to ice. The ice has nowhere to go but up—forming the pingo.

Extreme cold causes the surface of the tundra to shrink and crack. In spring, water fills the cracks. Later in the year, the water freezes, enlarging the cracks. In many places in the Arctic, such cracks form patterned shapes called polygons. From year to year, the cracks widen, making the polygons more distinct. If you fly over tundra, you're likely to see polygons clearly.

Bylot Island, Northwest Territories
Greenland*
Aappilattoq
Marble Island, Northwest Territories
Torngat Mountains, Labrador
Groswater Bay
Hudson Bay
Lake Superior
Lake Superior Provincial Park, Ontario
Shovel Point, Minnesota

*The official name of Greenland today is Kalaalit Nunaat.

STEPHEN J. KRASEMANN/DRK PHOTO

Seen from the air, a pattern marks the tundra like tiles on a floor (above). The many-sided figures, called polygons (PAHL-ih-gahnz), form as the ground freezes and thaws.

A pingo stands tall on the tundra in far northern Canada (below). It formed slowly after a lake filled up with dirt. Water under the dirt froze and expanded. The ice, blocked by frozen ground below, could only rise. Its cover of soil and plants now reaches up 157 feet (48 m).

FRED BRUEMMER

A Great Lake

In the 1600s, French explorers arrived on the shores of a huge lake they called *Lac Supérieur,* or Upper Lake. Chippewa Indians had already given the vast lake a title: *Gitchegome,* or Big Sea Water.

Lake Superior is not a sea, but it's large—the largest freshwater lake in the world. South Carolina would fit within its shores with room to spare. Enormous waves build in bad weather. Stormy Superior can be dangerous. The lake's history includes many shipwrecks.

Many people have worked hard to keep Lake Superior free of pollution. Miles of forested wilderness still surround the lake on both the Canadian and the United States shores. This wilderness remains today much as it was when American writer Henry Wadsworth Longfellow wrote a poem about an Indian boy named Hiawatha. Longfellow described the setting for the poem, called *The Song of Hiawatha,* at the start: "By the shores of Gitche Gumee, By the shining Big-Sea-Water. . . ."

At Shovel Point, in Minnesota, hikers watch Lake Superior pound its ancient rocky shore (right). Long ago, glaciers carved a deep trough in the Canadian Shield. Later, water filled the trough, forming the lake. Along the shore, geologists find evidence of volcanoes that erupted long before the glaciers came. The light-colored volcanic rocks in Lake Superior Provincial Park, in Ontario (above), are more than a billion years old.

The Old Land Of Newfoundland

Few roads enter the rocky wilderness of Labrador, the mainland part of Newfoundland. Icy Labrador Sea currents and cold winds from Hudson Bay contribute to the harsh climate. Few people live there.

Thousands of years ago, Ice Age glaciers carved this rugged landscape from ancient rock. When the ice crept across the area, only the tips of the mile-high mountains now called the Torngats showed above the glaciers. The glaciers carried away overlying soil and rock, exposing the ancient rocks that form the Canadian Shield. Shield rocks are some of the oldest on earth.

Rocks more than $3\frac{1}{2}$ billion years old are found both in the Torngats and on the west coast of Greenland. That's because Greenland once was attached to Canada. The two separated 50 million to 80 million years ago as the Atlantic Ocean formed. By studying the composition of these rocks, geologists learn more about what the earth was like in its early days.

If you travel to the high cliffs on the Labrador coast, you'll see puffins and many other seabirds. Labrador may not be very hospitable to human beings, but the rocky coast is a paradise for the birds that flock there to breed.

A waterfall plunges into a ravine in the Torngat Mountains of Labrador, in Canada (left). The remote coast nearby is home only to a few Inuit who fish for a living.

A rock in Groswater Bay provides a perch for puffins (right). Puffins spend the winter at sea, fishing and even sleeping among the waves. In the breeding season, thousands of them come ashore to nest along the Labrador coast.

Greenland: Island Under Ice

Greenland: the name sounds inviting. That's why Viking explorer Eric the Red used the name about a thousand years ago to describe the mostly ice-covered island. He hoped the name would attract settlers. They came, but Greenland's harsh environment eventually helped drive them away.

Greenlanders of today have about a hundred terms for ice. Each describes another form of the frozen substance. The many terms are useful, for ice covers most of Greenland year round. The ice sheet that blankets the island is the second-largest in the world. (Antarctica's is larger.) Glaciers flow into nearly every coastal bay and inlet.

Greenland is one of the least visited natural wonders of North America. Perhaps one day you'll make the long journey to the remote coast of the world's largest island.

JACK M. STEPHENS/BRUCE COLEMAN INC. (BELOW); N.G.S. PHOTOGRAPHER GEORGE MOBLEY (RIGHT)

Greenlanders row across an inlet dotted with icebergs (below). Greenland's glaciers spill about 15,000 large icebergs into the North Atlantic every year—as well as uncounted small ones. Only a small part of an iceberg shows above the waterline. In the clear water near shore, these boaters from the village of Aappilattoq can see the dangerous underwater parts of icebergs and avoid them. But in the open sea, the bulk of an iceberg hidden underwater is a threat to ships passing nearby.

Snow and ice lie atop an island off northwestern Greenland (above). For centuries, meltwater from glaciers has eroded notches in the shoreline cliffs. A few Inuit live in the remote areas of the north. But most people in Greenland have settled in small coastal towns in the southern part of their giant ice-capped island.

If Pikes Peak were on Greenland (left), the thickest part of Greenland's ice sheet would almost bury the 14,110-foot (4,301-m) mountain. The ice sheet—more than 2 miles (3 km) thick—is left over from the ice sheets that once covered much of North America.

ART BY GLORIA MARCONI, BASED ON ART IN *THE GREENLAND ICE CAP*, BY BØRGE FRISTRUP

ADDITIONAL READING

Readers may want to check the *National Geographic* or WORLD *Index* in a school or a public library for related articles and to refer to the following books. ("A" indicates a book for readers at the adult level.)

National Geographic Society Publications: *Alaska's Magnificent Parklands,* 1984. *Exploring Our Living Planet,* 1983 (A). *A Guide to Our Federal Lands,* 1984. *The New America's Wonderlands: Our National Parks,* 1980. *Our Continent: A Natural History of North America,* 1976 (A). *Our Violent Earth,* 1982.

Book Series: "Parks for People," by Ruth Radlauer (Childrens Press), includes books on these national parks: Acadia, Bryce Canyon, Denali, Everglades, Glacier, Grand Canyon, Grand Teton, Great Smoky Mountains, Mammoth Cave, Olympic, Yellowstone, Yosemite, Zion.

"The Story Behind the Scenery" (KC Publications) includes books on these sites or national parks: Acadia, Bryce Canyon, Canyonlands, Crater Lake, Death Valley, Mount McKinley, Everglades, Grand Canyon, Grand Teton, Great Smoky Mountains, Mount Rainier, Olympic, Yellowstone, Sonoran Desert, Yosemite, Zion.

General: Coburn, Doris, *A Spit is a Piece of Land: Landforms in the U. S. A.,* Julian Messner, 1978. Harris, David V., *The Geologic Story of the National Parks and Monuments,* John Wiley & Sons, 1980 (A). Landi, Val, *The Great American Countryside: A Traveller's Companion,* Macmillan, 1982. Livingston, John A., *Canada,* N. S. L. Natural Science of Canada, 1970. Matthews, William H. III, *Geology Made Simple,* Doubleday, 1982. Maynard, Christopher, *Exploring the Great Ice Age,* Franklin Watts, 1979. Redfern, Ron, *The Making of a Continent,* Times Books, 1983. Shimer, John A., *This Sculptured Earth: The Landscape of America,* Columbia University Press, 1959.

West Coast: Matthews, William H. III, *The Story of Volcanoes and Quakes,* Harvey House, 1969. Nixon, Hershell H. and Joan L., *Glaciers, Nature's Frozen Rivers,* Dodd, Mead, 1980. Nixon, Hershell H. and Joan L., *Volcanoes: Nature's Fireworks,* Dodd, Mead, 1978. Williams, Chuck, *Mount St. Helens: A Changing Landscape,* Graphic Arts Center, 1980 (A).

Basin and Range and Mexican Highlands: Behrens, June, and Pauline Brower, *Death Valley,* Childrens Press, 1980. Graham, Ada and Frank, *The Changing Desert,* Charles Scribner's, 1981. Young, Donald, *The Great American Desert,* Julian Messner, 1980.

Colorado Plateau: Ash, Sidney R., and David D. May, *Petrified Forest: The Story Behind the Scenery,* Petrified Forest Museum Association, 1969. Barnes, F. A., *Canyon Country Exploring,* Wasatch, 1978. Geerlings, Paul F., *Down the Grand Staircase, Grand Canyon's Living Adventure,* Grand Canyon Publications, 1980. Trimble, Stephen, *The Bright Edge: A Guide to the National Parks of the Colorado Plateau,* The Museum of Northern Arizona Press, 1979.

Rocky Mountains: Edwards, R. Yorke, *The Mountain Barrier,* N. S. L. Natural Science of Canada, 1970. Robinson, Bart, *Columbia Icefield— A Solitude of Ice,* Mountaineers-Books, 1981 (A).

Great Plains and Central Lowland: Allen, Durward L., *Life of Prairies and Plains,* McGraw-Hill, 1967. Allen, Robert Thomas, *The Great Lakes,* N. S. L. Natural Science of Canada, 1970. Clark, Champ, *The Badlands,* Time-Life Books, 1974 (A). Braithwaite, Max, *The Western Plains,* N. S. L. Natural Science of Canada, 1970. Russell, Dale A., *A Vanished World: The Dinosaurs of Western Canada,* National Museums of Canada, 1977.

Appalachian Highlands and Coastal Plain: Brooks, Maurice G., *The Appalachians,* Houghton Mifflin, 1965. Darell-Brown, Susan, *The Mississippi,* Silver Burdett, 1978. Randall, Peter, *Mount Washington: A Short History and Guide,* Down East Books, 1982.

Canadian Shield and Greenland: Adamson, Wendy Wriston, *Saving Lake Superior: A Story of Environmental Action,* Dillon, 1974. Anderson, Madelyn, *Greenland: Island at the Top of the World,* Dodd, Mead, 1983. Banks, Michael, *Greenland,* Rowman and Littlefield, 1975. Moon, Barbara, *The Canadian Shield,* N. S. L. Natural Science of Canada, 1970.

ADDRESSES FOR INFORMATION

If you want travel information about places in North America, write to the addresses below for Canada, Mexico, or the United States.

Canada: Canadian Government Office of Tourism, 1771 N Street N. W., Suite 200, Washington, D. C. 20036

Mexico: Mexican Government Tourism Office, 405 Park Avenue, Suite 1203, New York, New York 10022

United States: Alabama Bureau of Publicity & Information, 532 South Perry Street, Montgomery, Alabama 36104; **Alaska** Division of Tourism, Pouch E, Juneau, Alaska 99811; **Arizona** Office of Tourism, 3507 North Central Avenue, Suite 506, Phoenix, Arizona 85012; **Arkansas** Department of Parks & Tourism, One Capitol Mall, Little Rock, Arkansas 72201; **California** Office of Tourism, 1121 L Street, 1st Floor, Sacramento, California 95814; **Colorado** Office of Tourism, 5500 S. Syracuse Circle, Englewood, Colorado 80111; **Connecticut** Tourism Division, 210 Washington Street, Hartford, Connecticut 06106; **Delaware** State Travel Service, 99 Kings Highway, Dover, Delaware 19903; **District of Columbia:** see Washington, D. C.; **Florida** Visitor Inquiry Section, 126 Van Buren Street, Tallahassee, Florida 32301; **Georgia** Tourist Division, P. O. Box 1776, Atlanta, Georgia 30301; **Hawaii** Visitors Bureau, 2270 Kalakaua Avenue, Suite 801, Honolulu, Hawaii 96815; **Idaho** Tourism, State Capitol Building, Room 108, Boise, Idaho 83720; **Illinois** Travel Information Center, 310 North Michigan, Chicago, Illinois 60604; **Indiana** Tourism Division, One N. Capitol, Suite 700, Indianapolis, Indiana 46204; **Iowa** Tourism & Travel Division, Capitol Center, Des Moines, Iowa 50309; **Kansas** Tourist Division, 503 Kansas Avenue, 6th Floor, Topeka, Kansas 66603; **Kentucky** Department of Travel Development, Capital Plaza Tower, Frankfort, Kentucky 40601; **Louisiana** Office of Tourism, P. O. Box 44291, Baton Rouge, Louisiana 70804; **Maine** State Tourism Office, 189 State Street, Augusta, Maine 04333; **Maryland** Office of Tourist Development, 45 Calvert Street, Annapolis, Maryland 21401; **Massachusetts** Division of Tourism, 100 Cambridge Street, Boston, Massachusetts 02202; **Michigan** Travel Bureau, P. O. Box 30226, Lansing, Michigan 48909; **Minnesota** Travel Information Center, 240 Bremer Building, 419 North Robert Street, St. Paul, Minnesota 55101; **Mississippi** Division of Tourism, P. O. Box 849, Jackson, Mississippi 39205; **Missouri** Division of Tourism, P. O. Box 1055, Truman State Office Building, Jefferson City, Missouri 65102; **Montana** Travel Promotion Bureau, 1424 Ninth Avenue, Helena, Montana 59620; **Nebraska** Division of Travel & Tourism, P. O. Box 94666, Lincoln, Nebraska 68509; **Nevada** Commission on Tourism, Capitol Complex, Carson City, Nevada 89710; **New Hampshire** Office of Vacation Travel, Box 856, Concord, New Hamphire 03301; **New Jersey** Division of Travel & Tourism, CN 826, Trenton, New Jersey 08625; **New Mexico** Tourism & Travel Division, Bataan Memorial Building, Santa Fe, New Mexico 87503; **New York** Division of Tourism Development, 1 Commerce Plaza, Albany, New York 12245; **North Carolina** Travel & Tourism Division, 430 North Salisbury Street, Raleigh, North Carolina 27611; **North Dakota** Tourism Promotion Division, Capitol Grounds, Bismarck, North Dakota 58505; **Ohio** Office of Travel & Tourism, P. O. Box 1001, Columbus, Ohio 43216; **Oklahoma** Tourism & Recreation Department, 500 Will Rogers Building, Oklahoma City, Oklahoma 73105; **Oregon** Tourism Division, 595 Cottage Street N. E., Salem, Oregon 97310; **Pennsylvania** Bureau of Travel Development, 416 Forum Building, Harrisburg, Pennsylvania 17120; **Rhode Island** Tourist Promotion Division, 7 Jackson Walkway, Providence, Rhode Island 02903; **South Carolina** Department of Parks, Recreation & Tourism, 1205 Pendleton Street, Suite 110, Columbia, South Carolina 29201; **South Dakota** Division of Tourism, P. O. Box 6000, Pierre, South Dakota 57501; **Tennessee** Department of Tourist Development, P. O. Box 23170, Nashville, Tennessee 37202; **Texas** Travel & Information Division, P. O. Box 5064, Austin, Texas 78763; **Utah** Travel Council, Council Hall/Capitol Hill, Salt Lake City, Utah 84114; **Vermont** Travel Division, 134 State Street, Montpelier, Vermont 05602; **Virginia** Division of Tourism, 202 North Ninth Street, Suite 500, Richmond, Virginia 23219; **Washington** Tourism Development Division, 101 General Administration Building, Olympia, Washington 98504; **Washington, D. C.,** Convention & Visitors Association, 1575 Eye Street N. W., Suite 250, Washington, D. C. 20005; **West Virginia** Travel Development, Building 6, Room B-564, Charleston, West Virginia 25305; **Wisconsin** Division of Tourism, P. O. Box 7606, Madison, Wisconsin 53707; **Wyoming** Travel Commission, Frank Norris Jr. Travel Center, Cheyenne, Wyoming 82002

INDEX

Bold type refers to illustrations;
regular type refers to text.

EDUCATIONAL CONSULTANTS

Peter B. Stifel, Ph.D., Professor of Geology,
  University of Maryland; William H. Matthews III, Ph.D.,
  Regents Professor of Geology, Lamar University, *Chief Consultants*
Glenn O. Blough, LL.D., Emeritus Professor of Education,
  University of Maryland, *Educational Consultant*
Nicholas J. Long, Ph.D., *Consulting Psychologist*
Joan Myers, *Reading Consultant*
Phyllis G. Sidorsky, *Consulting Librarian*

The Special Publications and School Services Division is also grateful to the individuals and institutions named or quoted within the text and to those cited here for their generous assistance:

Judith Abarbanel, Colorado Outward Bound School; Douglas D. Anderson, Brown University; Joan Anzelmo, Roderick Hutchinson, Amy Vanderbilt, Yellowstone National Park; Albert G. Ballert, Michael J. Donahue, Great Lakes Commission; F. A. Barnes; David Biederman, Jasper National Park; Sherma E. Bierhaus, Anna Marie Fender, Arches National Park; R. G. Blackadar, W. C. Morgan, Geological Survey of Canada; Ray Bonenberg, Lake Superior Provincial Park; John Carter, Nebraska State Historical Society; Edwin H. Colbert, Museum of Northern Arizona; Susan Colclazer, L. Edward Gastellum, Petrified Forest National Park; Harold Coss, Saguaro National Monument; Doug Cuillard, Denali National Park and Preserve; Lewis B. Cutliff, Mammoth Cave National Park; Don DeFoe, Great Smoky Mountains National Park; Bill Dengler, Mount Rainier National Park.

Elwood L. Dillman, Public Works Canada; Brenda Filippelli, Prima County Parks and Recreation; Karene Forman, Glacier National Park; Emmett Foster, Pike and San Isobel National Forest; David Gaines, Irene Mandelbaum, Mono Lake Committee; James Gale, Mount St. Helens National Volcanic Monument; Mary Elizabeth Gale, Jack O'Brien, Grand Canyon National Park; Greg H. Gordon, Mount Washington Observatory; James Griffin, John Wilbrecht, National Elk Refuge, U. S. Fish and Wildlife Service; Don L. Halvorson, University of North Dakota; Jennifer Hartley, Yosemite National Park; Judi Hebbring, National Buffalo Association; Chris Helms, Arizona–Sonora Desert Museum; Susan Holler, Robert Woody, Cape Hatteras National Seashore; Victor L. Jackson, Zion National Park; Ronal Kerbo, Carlsbad Caverns National Park; Mike Keuss, U. S. Army Corps of Engineers; Rodney Klein, Happy Trails, Inc.; Curt Kraft, Calaveras Big Trees State Park; Chester C. Langway, Jr., State University of New York at Buffalo; B. C. Lieff, Waterton Lakes National Park; Margaret Littlejohn, Bryce Canyon National Park; Nancy Maday, Pikes Peak Library District; Dave McGinnis, Badlands National Park; Gregg Morgan, Bureau of Land Management; David K. Morris, Katmai National Park and Preserve; Virgil Olson, Death Valley National Monument.

John J. Palmer, Sequoia and Kings Canyon National Parks; Keith Parlette, Schoellkopf Geological Museum; C. E. Peach, Fundy Gypsum Company, Ltd.; Stan Riggs, East Carolina University; Vicky Scharlau-Nelson, State of Washington Department of Agriculture; Robert L. Schultz, Great Sand Dunes National Monument; Wendy Scratch, U. S. Geological Survey; Art Seamans, Hells Canyon National Recreation Area; Patricia Simmons, Bureau of Indian Affairs; Jeffrey A. Smith, The American Waterways Operators, Inc.; Patrick Smith, Grand Teton National Park; Ned Therrien, White Mountain National Forest; R. Gregory Thompson, U. S. Forest Service; Ron D. Thoreson, Canyonlands National Park; Pat Tolle, Everglades National Park; Jim Vollmershausen, Banff National Park; Robert J. Walker, Fundy National Park; John A. Walper, Dinosaur Provincial Park; Carl Wamboldt, Montana State University; Ronald Warfield, Crater Lake National Park; Fred White, Navajo Tribal Council; Lois Winter, Acadia National Park.

Composition for NATURAL WONDERS OF NORTH AMERICA by National Geographic's Photographic Services, Carl M. Shrader, Director; Lawrence F. Ludwig, Assistant Director. Printed and bound by Holladay-Tyler Printing Corp., Rockville, Md. Color separations by the Lanman-Progressive Co., Washington, D. C.; Lincoln Graphics, Inc., Cherry Hill, N.J.; NEC, Inc., Nashville, Tenn. FAR-OUT FUN! printed by McCollum Press, Inc., Rockville, Md. *Classroom Activities* produced by Mazer Corp., Dayton, Ohio.

Library of Congress CIP Data

O'Neill, Catherine, 1950-
    Natural wonders of North America.
    (Books for world explorers)
    Bibliography: p.
    Includes index.
    1. Geology—North America. 2. Landforms—North America.
I. Title. II. Series.
QE71.054   1984   557   84-16614
ISBN 0-87044-514-6
ISBN 0-87044-519-7 (library edition)

NATURAL WONDERS OF NORTH AMERICA

by Catherine O'Neill

PUBLISHED BY
THE NATIONAL GEOGRAPHIC SOCIETY
WASHINGTON, D. C.

Gilbert M. Grosvenor, *President*
Melvin M. Payne, *Chairman of the Board*
Owen R. Anderson, *Executive Vice President*
Robert L. Breeden, *Vice President,
Publications and Educational Media*

PREPARED BY THE SPECIAL PUBLICATIONS
AND SCHOOL SERVICES DIVISION

Donald J. Crump, *Director*
Philip B. Silcott, *Associate Director*
William L. Allen, *Assistant Director*

BOOKS FOR WORLD EXPLORERS
Ralph Gray, *Editor*
Pat Robbins, *Managing Editor*
Ursula Perrin Vosseler, *Art Director*

STAFF FOR *NATURAL WONDERS OF NORTH AMERICA*
Roger B. Hirschland, *Managing Editor*
Dennis R. Dimick, *Picture Editor*
Lynette R. Ruschak, *Designer*
Carolinda Hill, Jennifer A. Kirkpatrick, Suzanne
  Nave Patrick, *Researchers*
Lori E. Davie, Katherine R. Leitch, *Editorial
  Assistants*
Artemis S. Lampathakis, *Illustrations Assistant*
Janet A. Dustin, *Art Secretary*
John D. Garst, Jr., Peter J. Balch, and Joseph F.
  Ochlak, *Locator-map Research and Production*
Gloria Marconi, *Spot Art*

STAFF FOR *FAR-OUT FUN!*: Patricia N. Holland, *Project Editor;*
Martha C. Christian, *Text Editor;* Eleanor Shannahan,
Game Board Editor; Ursula Perrin Vosseler, *Designer;*
Barbara Brownell, Jennifer A. Kirkpatrick, Suzanne
Nave Patrick, *Researchers;* Loel Barr, *Artist*

ENGRAVING, PRINTING, AND PRODUCT MANUFACTURE: Robert W.
Messer, *Manager;* George V. White, *Production Manager;* Mary A. Bennett, *Production Project Manager;* Mark
R. Dunlevy, David V. Showers, Gregory Storer, George J.
Zeller, Jr., *Assistant Production Managers;* Julia F.
Warner, *Production Staff Assistant*

STAFF ASSISTANTS: Mary Evelyn Anderson, Nancy F. Berry,
Elizabeth A. Brazerol, Dianne T. Craven, Susan Crosman, Carol R. Curtis, Mary Elizabeth Davis, Rosamund
Garner, Bernadette L. Grigonis, Nancy J. Harvey, Joan
Hurst, Cleo Petroff, Sheryl A. Prohovich, Nancy E. Simson, Pamela Black Townsend, Virginia A. Williams

MARKET RESEARCH: Mark W. Brown, Joseph S. Fowler,
Carrla L. Holmes, Meg McElligott Kieffer, Susan D.
Snell, Barbara G. Steinwurtzel

INDEX: Jeffrey A. Brown